APPLICANT INTERVIEW PREPARATION

APPLICANT INTERVIEW PREPARATION

Practical Coaching for Today

Warren S. Cook

AUTHORITY MEDIA GROUP
NEWARK, DELAWARE

Authority Media Group
2035 Sunset Lake Road #B2
Newark, DE 19702
www.authoritymediagroup.com

Ordering Information:
Quantity sales. Special discounts are available on quantity purchase by corporations, associations, and others. For details, contact the "Special Sales Department" at the address above.

Supplemental material for this book is available at the author's website: www.symbiancehr.net

Library of Congress Catalog Number: 2016938926

Applicant Interview Preparation / Warren S. Cook. -- 1st ed.

ISBN   978-0-9909955-2-4

This book is dedicated to Dr. Martin Kessel, my mentor, my friend, and the most caring man I have ever met.

CONTENTS

ACKNOWLEDGEMENTS

Thank you to my loving wife Jennifer, and my children Brett, Nicholas, Heather, and Dominick for their love and support empowering me to write this book.

CHAPTER ONE

PURPOSE OF THIS BOOK

Perhaps you just finished high school and are hoping to land your first job at a local store. Maybe you are receiving your degree soon from a college or university and have begun pursuing employment opportunities at a large corporation. Then again, you may just be in a dead end job now looking to secure your dream job. For many who are unemployed or underemployed, you know you are more than capable of securing that next great position to take care of yourself and your loved ones but there is something that continues to prevent you from achieving this goal. It is a frustrating and stressful process.

Throughout your life you will be forced to participate in a series of events that may be unfamiliar or unreasonable to you in the pursuit of a new job, the job application and interview process. What is often most difficult about these events is the loss of control by the applicant and the placement of your future in the hands of the employer for whom you wish to work.

The information in this book will provide you valuable insight into the recruitment process from the perspective and experience of a human capital strategist and human resource leader. After reading this book you will be more prepared for each stage of the recruitment process, and you will have the guidance to become more introspective of your capabilities which can aid you in enhancing your resume and responding to questions during an interview. Your confidence level will improve as you learn strategies and techniques to execute before, during, and after the interview to regain as much control of the process as possible.

When considering your competence and your experience this content will empower you to master the art of articulation. Many applicants do not get rejected because they lack the necessary skills for a position, rather they are rejected due to their failure to effectively and efficiently articulate to the interviewer or panel their knowledge, skills, abilities, competencies and experience.

For over twenty years I watched one applicant after another present an application and resume that lacked true substance or representation of what the individual was capable of. Too often a dedicated individual simply failed to articulate any experience or competence that was beautifully outlined in a resume. Many applicants attempt to use buzz words and clichés to satisfy the inquiry presented to them by the employer, which resulted in utter failure on their part.

These experiences by applicants need to come to an end. There is minimal emphasis in the education system on the skills necessary to be successful through the recruitment process. Therefore, it is time to educate and support our community and society by providing this valuable information to position more individuals to achieve greater success in their career pursuits.

CHAPTER TWO

WHY INTERVIEW PREPARATION?

The employer is prepared, shouldn't you be? Think about it this way, the employer has spent time, resources, and effort in training their supervisors and managers for hours and hours on their recruitment process, their style of interviewing, how to review a resume, what questions to ask, and how to remain legally compliant. The deck is already stacked against you, therefore to achieve your goal of a job offer you too need to become prepared.

Organizations often have very little room for failure in a recruitment process. If you take a moment to consider the large investment of time and resources necessary to post a position, screen applications and review resumes, conduct numerous rounds of interviews with key decision makers, and have staff coordinate all of this with applicants you will recognize that being organized and prepared to execute a recruitment process is costly. Preparation and training is a critical success factor for an organization seeking to make a good hire.

Clearly a business has various steps in their processes, and these are different from one employer to another. What you need to recognize and understand is that interview preparation is not just about learning what to say in the interview, it is about gaining a deeper competence in the entire systemic process so that you are prepared at each and every stage of the process.

By reading this book you will learn strategies that will help you master each stage of the recruitment process as the applicant. This practical and easy to understand information will prepare you for your next interview and you will gain greater confidence in achieving your goals.

CHAPTER THREE

SELECTION PROCESSES AND APPLICANT TRACKING SYSTEMS

Here is where the paradigm shift in your thinking begins to take place. I start with some background and information about why an employer is conducting an interview process to begin with. Have you ever even thought about it, or do you take it for granted that an interview is just something that happens?

Employers need to identify and hire the most qualified applicant for their vacancy. They spend a great deal of time and resources during the recruitment process and during the onboarding process to select, hire, train, and develop an individual to be successful in their organization and to aid them in achieving their business goals. When a position is posted, it is the employers responsibility to narrow down the applicant pool to that one individual they plan to hire. Therefore, I need you to think about the recruitment process like a funnel. However, what most people believe is the employer is interviewing so they can hire them. Quite the contrary, a recruitment process, like a funnel, is designed to eliminate as many unqualified applicants as possible, and then to narrow down the qualified applicant pool to the most qualified, and then ultimately to the successful applicant. So the process is a tool to eliminate people, not be inclusive. If you think about how some organizations today receive thousands of applications a month for their vacancies, there is no way anyone can read and review all of the applications and determine who needs to be interviewed. This is one catalyst for the birth of an applicant tracking system (ATS).

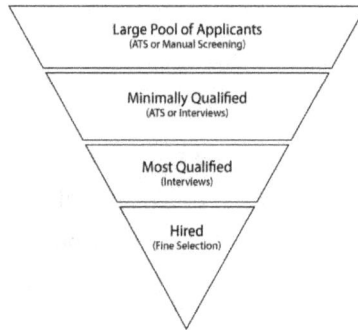

Large Pool of Applicants
(ATS or Manual Screening)

Minimally Qualified
(ATS or Interviews)

Most Qualified
(Interviews)

Hired
(Fine Selection)

Small businesses often still have a very relaxed and informal recruitment process. These organizations often rely on networking and word of mouth to find people to benefit their growth and expansion efforts. Once they find someone they are interested in, a quick chat with the owner often lands the individual the job. Generally, these types of businesses do not have any formal application process, may not even request a resume, and will simply have you meet with members of their team and make a decision.

From a process perspective, the strategies presented here will aid you in your conversations with these organizations and place you in a more confident and effective position to secure the job. What you need to understand is there will be minimal structure to the process, and the interviews may expand far outside of what is legal or complaint for an employer to be asking an applicant during the recruitment process.

When you begin your job search, and you identify an organization that requests you to complete and submit an application and resume online, there are two types of application processes that could take place. The first is the more rudimentary process of a website submission that is in reality a form or template that allows a visitor to attach documents and transmit to the employer by way of an email. Even if the website appears to be a form you are completing, if you are simply attaching documents and submitting, you are most likely completing an application process through email. What does this mean for you? Well it means that someone at the employer is manually reviewing and screening all of the submissions. It also means there may be no formal or structured screening criteria taking place prior to an individual making the decision. This can be beneficial for you if your resume is aesthetically pleasing and has met the surface requirements of the organization's screener. This process is very simple, however there is often no mechanism for you to check on the status of the application or recruitment process. You also may not get any other communication from the employer and wonder what is going on for quite some time unless you follow up directly through other means of communication.

Now before we learn about an ATS, we also want you to understand another catalyst for the development of formal and structured tracking systems. One word – compliance.

Compliance comes in many forms, but however you look at it there have been organizations that have discriminated against individuals for a variety of reasons that eventually led to both federal and state legislation governing hiring and personnel practices in the United States of America. While this book is not going to cover the laws in any depth it is important for you to understand which laws to research if you decide you want to learn more about your rights and what employers cannot and should not ask you during the process. The most effective way presently to gain this knowledge is to review the Department of Labors' (DOL) internet website specifically pertaining to discrimination and employment laws. The Equal Employment Opportunity Commission (EEOC) is the regulatory body with the authority to monitor and investigate complaints related to discrimination and employment laws. Take steps to be well informed as to your rights so that you can participate in the recruitment process as an applicant knowledgeable and confident of what is acceptable. Also know that there is a higher level of regulatory compliance expectations for federal government contractors, and if you are applying for a position with such an entity, the government agency that regulates their activities in addition to the DOL is the Office of Federal Contract Compliance Programs.

What does all of this mean for the recruitment process and you? The application process will be different because there will be a comprehensive ATS in place that you have to use in order to apply. You may have already experienced this type of application process. If you have ever had to create a profile, complete an online form that became the application, and then attach documents such as your resume, cover letter, and any reference letters then you have experienced an ATS.

The other key part of this type of system is the compliance standards it provides the employer. This means the system is designed to ensure various compliance components are executed to later aid the employer with the regulatory reporting such as their annual Equal Employment Opportunity report to the EEOC. As mentioned earlier, government contractors have a higher regulatory obligation which includes the development and maintenance of Affirmative Action Programs and Plans. These plans require specific reports such as applicant pools, applicant flow, adverse impact analysis, and much more. Because of these requirements, you will notice there will be a part of the application process in which you are requested to provide your gender, race, any disability status, and any veteran status. While these items are not mandatory to apply, you can feel comfortable reporting them honestly and accurately, because the ATS technology itself is designed to prevent human resources and hiring managers from seeing any of this information individually. Instead, the technology culminates the data and generates summary information for government reporting.

Another aspect of an ATS is the capability to use technology to systematically, consistently, and in a compliant manner narrow down the applicant pool. How does this affect you? As you complete the online application, you will be presented with both general and then more specific questions related directly to the performance of the essential functions of the position, and the minimum and preferred qualifications. The system, not a person, will be the first line of defense for the employer in screening out applicants that don't make the cut. What you also need to know is the employer develops and implements these screening questions to save time and resources during the process.

What this means for you is that you must recognize the necessity in completing all aspects of the ATS presented to you in the process. Failure to do so could eliminate you from the process or prevent you from being considered as an applicant for the position. These systems are not all user friendly, sometimes they time out, and they all take a great deal of time to complete.

There are various strategies you will want to implement when applying for positions online, including preparation of the application, your resume, cover letter, and references. Here is a brief list of steps to prepare for these activities, additional information will be covered in detail in Chapters 7 & 8

.

- Prepare a PDF version of your current resume for submissions online. This prevents tampering with your information.
- Have your resume open and available to you while completing the application so you can cut and paste when necessary for each position you have held.
- Have a text only version of your resume open and available for pasting into the ATS.
- Document your username and password so you can access the submitted application, and this employer's system in the future.
- Complete all required sections of the online application.

- Save your progress as you go in the event of a lost connection or the system timing out.
- Have a PDF version of your cover letter ready to attach, and be sure it is specific to the position you are applying for.
- Have 3 professional and 3 personal references handy when you begin the application process. Not all systems ask for it, but you want to be ready if they do.

If you are wondering, why you should have a copy of a text only version of your resume available you are not alone but here is where the wisdom and insight of this book comes into play. Most ATS systems have expansive capabilities, however many businesses cannot afford to turn on and implement all of the functionality. When you upload and attach your resume as a document or PDF, with all of the pretty formatting, the ATS simply stores the file with your user account for retrieval by the business. What the ATS does not do in most circumstances, is convert the uploaded file into a searchable text file. So what does this mean for you? Here is an example, you are an accountant, and you apply to ABC Company through their ATS. You attach your resume to the online application and you are qualified and ultimately interviewed. Unfortunately, you are not hired at this time but three months later the employer posts a new vacancy for an accountant position. The employer cannot leverage the power of their ATS in finding you as a former applicant unless they have search capabilities. Since most organizations do not implement this depth of functionality, they either start the process from scratch all over not benefiting from prior interested applicants, or they turn on the ability to capture a text version of your resume. This means that when our accountant applicant applied online, if they took advantage of the opportunity to both attach a resume or document and pasted a text only version into the system, they increased their chances of getting contacted by the employer for the new opening.

The final strategy for applicant tracking systems is making sure you have a professional and consistent naming convention for all of your electronic files. What I recommend is each file be named as follows:

- Last Name, First Initial, Document Type, Date
- DoeJ Resume mm-dd-yy
- DoeJ Cover Letter mm-dd-yy
- DoeJ References mm-dd-yy

Be very cognizant of every step in the process including every detail from the name and type of files you submit to the content you share. Once you begin the application process you are giving the employer organization a magnifying glass into who you are professionally and as a person. Do not lose sight of this in anything you do. This book will continue to provide tips and strategies of how to retain as much control as possible and leverage all advantages you can to position yourself for success in getting the interview and then presenting yourself in the most effective manner during the interview in achievement of the real goal, the job offer.

CHAPTER FOUR

TYPES OF INTERVIEWS

Employers have a wide range of choices when it comes to how they interview applicants for their vacant positions. These options are directly related to the purpose and goal of the interview at the various stages of the interview process. The interview is a tactical step in a strategic process of narrowing down an applicant pool to the most qualified applicants. We will review nine different types of interviews that you may experience based on the stage and type of position for which you are applying for. Not every employer uses these strategies in a similar fashion, and not all human resource departments execute the recruitment process the same way. There are certainly best practices and industry norms, however as long as the actual recruitment process is compliant, there is little in the form of strict guidelines for how the selection process for a vacant position must be done. This chapter will provide insight into the goals and purpose of the interview style selected for any particular situation and increase your opportunity to appropriately prepare for the event.

Covered in this chapter is screening, phone interview, one-on-one, panel, general content, competency content, stress, role play, and presentation types of interviews. In this chapter I explain how and when an organization might use each type of interview so expectations are appropriate and execution is more effective for you as the applicant.

Screening

For many organizations there is a lapse in time from when a position is posted, to the collection of applications, through to the actual review and assessment of applicants. Because of this, it is often prudent for an employer to take steps to ensure each of their selected applicants are (1) still interested in the opportunity; (2) still available to interview; (3) understands the qualification requirements; and (4) understands the salary and location information. Therefore, when you receive an email or telephone call from a potential employer and it is brief and concise on these topics, the event you just experienced is a telephone screen. The caller is tasked with making sure you are still an active applicant and asks a few specific questions to confirm you are the applicant. The screener may also request availability if preparing to offer you an interview.

The key strategy in handling these calls is to recognize this is not a full interview but a critical screening to set you up for the interview. Be clear, confident, and accurate with your responses because this is the path to the next step in the process. Demonstrate flexibility for the opportunity while using this interaction with a representative of the employer to ask questions and gather information. Remember, the recruitment process affords both employer and applicant to learn about the other so that an informed decision can be made at the conclusion of the process. Do not be surprised if the screener is not very informed about the position, the organization, who you will be interviewing with, or any other information you are seeking. It is common for this function to be outsourced to third party independent recruiters or staffing firms by larger corporations. It is also common for an individual to have the role of screener at a company without being provided any level of details of the role for the sole purposes noted earlier in verifying the applicant is still viable. The key here is to provide the caller information that will aid you in advancing in the process while obtaining any and all information you can during the call. Sometimes you will not hear back from an employer after the screener call, this is not at all unusual but it is frustrating and disappointing. If the screener determines from your responses that your understanding of the role, location, salary, or any other aspect is inconsistent with your application, they may discount you from the process, and you will never know the details or reasons why. This is why it is critically important to be consistent with your application and resume information to employers so that information you present off the cuff on a screening call will match what you submitted on the application. Do not misrepresent your background, experience, or other factors on an application because if the employer suspects such you may be discarded from the applicant pool and never know what happened.

Telephone Interview

Effective and efficient, the telephone interview is generally the first interaction between the applicant and a member of the employer organization who has influence in the selection process. Do not be misled into thinking a telephone interview is not formal or has little to do with a face to face interview or an in person interview. The interviewer may be a manager or supervisor, the hiring manager, a member of the human resources staff, or anyone who is knowledgeable in the needs of the organization and the subject matter expertise to discern which applicants are not qualified to proceed in the process.

Strategically as an applicant, you want to be as prepared as possible for this type of interview, because it will make or break your chances of advancing in the process. When possible, request the interview be scheduled so you are not caught off guard by an unexpected call from an employer seeking to interview you on the spot. This approach lacks professionalism and care for the applicant, and provides insight into how employees may be treated at that particular company.

It is wise to have a copy of your application and resume with you during the interview to reference and rely on so you are not trying to remember everything. After reviewing later chapters in this book you will also want to have note cards prepared for cues on your responses and your questions for the interviewer. You will want to ensure you are in a confidential location that limits any distractions or interruptions, and that when taking a call on a cellular phone you have planned ahead to ensure reception and battery life.

Face to Face Interview

An employer will either have a telephone interview as step one of the interview process or skip and move directly to an interview in which you have the opportunity to meet an individual from the organization and discuss your background and experience. This is often referred to in industry as the formal interview, although as previously noted the telephone interview, or with current technology the video interview is just as formal and critical to be prepared for in the process.

What you need to know about the face to face process is that the employer has spent time planning this stage very carefully. There are key subject matter experts used in face to face interviews which translates into important information for you in preparing and executing the interview with the best results. This type of interview can happen two different ways; (1) you may meet with individual members of the employer at different times and possibly even on different dates; or (2) you may meet with a group or panel of individuals from the employer. There are generally reasons for how the employer has selected to execute the recruitment process, and what is explained next is the strategy and purpose of these styles.

Face to Face Interview (One-on-One)

Employers want to ensure they hire the most qualified applicant for the position, and this requires an examination and review of qualifications, experience, competency, culture fit, and a host of other characteristics that align the applicant with the position and organization. Expect to have several sessions ranging in duration with a manager or supervisor of the position or a similar position with the organization, a human resource professional, and a technical subject matter expert.

The reason for the various interviews as compared to a panel interview is often due to availability on the side of the employer. It is not always easy to coordinate all of the key individuals at the same time and date for interviews, resulting in an often extended process for the employer and a somewhat disjointed process for the applicant. Many organizations are extremely effective with this approach, and will use the panel style of interview during parts of the process, and one-on-one style for other parts. For example, you may meet with human resources to review the position, general qualifications, discuss benefits, salary information, and culture fit. Next you may meet with one or several subject matter experts who ask you a variety of questions related to the technical aspects of the position. Finally, your interview day may be wrapped up with the hiring manager, who relies on the other steps of the process for insight into final decision-making. There are pros and cons for the applicant with this process for which this insight will prepare you for maximizing your chances of success during the interviews.

First, the potential obstacles and challenges for the applicant which can hinder or damage your chances for advancement are inherent in the employer's choice of this approach. Consider for a moment that you may be required in a process like this to tell "your story" several times to an employer who is evaluating your consistency and accuracy in what you present. As the employer will be taking notes in each interview and comparing later, the applicant must be on guard to not alter or change their representation of skills, abilities, experience, etc. to each interviewer. Rest assured the interview team will be sharing notes and information in order to make their decision. Since most people like to break the ice and get comfortable for an interview, time is lost in actually presenting your capabilities to the interviewer as time is wasted with introductions numerous times. Often the applicant attempts to discern what the interviewer is looking for based on their title and questions, altering responses subconsciously in hopes to satisfy the interviewer.

Finally, each interviewer will hear your responses through a different filter, and if not well trained as an interviewer there are risks in misinterpreting answers from the applicant. This sounds like a problem for the employer, but it is actually a greater problem for the applicant because if the interview team cannot agree on what they heard and observed there is an increased chance in the applicant being rejected from the process. All of these behaviors and situations are real obstacles to your success in the process. All interview styles have obstacles for the applicant, which is why you are reading this book, to gain the insight and strategies for overcoming the challenges and achieving success.

The benefits for the applicant in separate interviews is exposure to different individuals with different goals and views of a successful applicant. Organizations are very hopeful that the interview team is aligned with the needs of the role, but when they are isolated with an applicant, personal and professional bias enters the process and this can be used to your advantage by demonstrating you meet the needs of the particular interviewer in each session. Another benefit to a process like this is the applicant's opportunity to share more than they could in one panel setting. Think about it this way, you may have three hours of interviewing in which to present who you are and what you are capable of, even if spun differently based on the questions asked in each session, or one hour with a panel in which the questions are designed to meet the needs of all the participants in the process. Use this insight to your advantage and make the most out of the process put before you.

Face to Face Interview (Panel)

In contrast to the separate sessions noted already, organizations recognize they can leverage the time, resources, and effort in their recruitment process by coordinating panel interviews for selection activities. Recognize that this approach may be used for a variety of reasons, some of which include efficiency, timeliness, volume of applicants, training of managers, and compliance. In fact, some employers establish interview panels as a result of mandatory compliance obligations or concerns of equitable hiring practices. For example, if leadership recognizes a lack of diverse hiring from applicant pools that contain diverse applicants, they may institute a requirement on interview panels to enhance their confidence in legal recruiting practices. What this means for you is that human resources will most likely be involved in the panel, and the panel itself will consist of individuals of different genders and races. When all is said and done what the applicant needs to understand is there is going to be a number of panel members all listening to each and every word spoken during the interview in an effort to discern capabilities and experience necessary to be successful in the role. Equally important is the applicant will have only a limited amount of time to interview with the panel, which is often less time than when interviews are done separately.

While this type of interview is often the most intimidating, preparing yourself for the interview will nullify any advantage the employer believes it has over you due to understanding how to best leverage the event to your advantage. Note that in a panel interview you are able to demonstrate competence and present your capabilities to several people at once who will have the difficult task of determining if you provided satisfactory responses to their questions. Strategies presented later in this book will enhance your ability to articulate and present who you are during this type of interview taking advantage of the larger captivated audience before you.

General Interview

In the context of interview style and type, the aforementioned interviews focus heavily on the method in which the interview is conducted. The explanation of a general interview and the other types to follow are designed to expand your knowledge on the format of the interview and what you can expect the content and structure to be for the interview event.

In a general interview the context of the questions will often be focused on general position requirements, background and experience, culture fit and personality match with the interviewer and company. Often these interviews include discussion about the company benefit programs, compensation, company history and goals, and other high level topics that evaluate your fit for a role with the company, but rarely dive into the core competencies and necessary capabilities to be effective and successful in the role. Human resource professionals are often tasked with this step of the process, as they are uniquely qualified to evaluate an applicant and determine how they would assimilate into the workforce and the role effectively to meet business goals. This is not to discount the technical competence of human resource professionals, but organizations often use technical subject matter experts for other styles of interviews which I present next.

Competency Interview

When you apply for a position and receive communication that you will be interviewing with the company's expert in that area you can be confident the style of interview you are going to have is a competency based interview. Industry refers to this often as the "technical" interview, and is heavily used in the life sciences and technology fields in which specialized training, experience, or knowledge is necessary to perform the essential functions of a role. For example, when an applicant applies for a position as a laboratory chemist, a human resource professional may conduct a general interview to get the process started, but a senior level experienced chemist will conduct the competence interview necessary to determine if the applicant really has the knowledge, skills, and abilities to perform the role of laboratory chemist at their organization. Another simple example is a computer programmer, in which a senior level programming developer or architect may conduct this style of interview.

What the applicant needs to understand is the interview will be drastically different from a general interview. The interviewer may spend minimal time with pleasantries and jump right into technical questions to determine what you know. There is nothing to worry about with this type of interview if you have applied for a position for which you are actually qualified, and you apply the strategies and techniques of this book in preparing for the interview.

Stress Interview

If you have ever been scheduled for an interview at 9:00 A.M. and sat waiting until almost 9:30 A.M. to get started you would probably be surprised to know that in some organizations, this may have been intentional to evaluate how you handle stress. Another example of a stress style interview is one in which the interview will be interrupted several times allowing the interviewer to observe how you handle the interruptions. Organizations that analyze and reflect on the psychological aspects of the position for which you are applying may have identified certain stressors or events that cause traumatic response and design a method to determine how well an applicant can handle these situations. Even something as simple as dealing with the public may be cause for an employer to design a situation or set of questions for the applicant to aid in the evaluation of behaviors for success. One way to do this by the interviewer is to have the applicant role play, which we cover next. Do not assume, however, that any changes in the interview, a delay, or an interruption is a demonstration of a stress interview. To deal with unexpected change an employer may advise an applicant they will be interviewing with a supervisor and then a different individual conducts the interview. These are not used regularly and take careful planning and execution to be effective. Remember that the interview itself must be tied back to the performance of the essential functions of the position to be a compliant process.

Role Play

When applying to be in a play or show, this may be the most enjoyable type of interview style for an applicant. For the main stream majority of applicants, it may be traumatic and stifling to learn that the interview being conducted will include role playing with the interviewer or interview panel. This type of interview is extremely effective and beneficial during the recruiting process especially when the organization uses behavioral interviewing techniques. It is one thing for an applicant to tell the interviewer they can do something; it is something else for the applicant to prove it. Do not let this reality scare you, as the purpose of explaining all of this to you as an applicant is to prepare you for what is going to happen and give you the tools and strategies to excel during an interview to achieve your goal of receiving an offer.

Role play interviewing involves the employer presenting the applicant a situation and requesting that the applicant do something with the situation. This is not to be confused with testing, such as being asked to take a computer test to complete a task. Testing is not something covered in this book since it is not technically an interview, it is a test. However, be cautious when being asked to take a test by a potential employer, and ask the organization if the test has been determined compliant through a validation study for the position for which it is being used.

Once you identify the style of interview being used is a role play, prepare yourself for not only carrying out the instructions but for intentional resistance from the interviewer to whatever you do. This type of interview is designed to throw the applicant obstacles and challenges real time to observe reaction. This simulates what might really happen in the role you applied for, and is very appropriate in determining an applicant's capabilities in demonstrating the necessary competence for the role.

What you need to know is what not to do in this situation, so here are several tips to make your role play most successful. Listen carefully, and take notes to ensure you captured the key points of the situation. Verify what you heard from the interviewer before you begin, but be cautious about asking questions about the scenario because it may reflect lack of experience or knowledge in the skill being observed. Do not explain to the interviewer what you "would do" or "would say" but rather actually say it or do it. Interact with the interviewer as if they were the character in their scenario they described to you. Execute your actions the same way you would if the scenario really happened once you worked there or how you have in your current or prior position.

There are a few tips to apply when participating in a role play to avoid interruptions, inconsistent presentation, or failing to present your competence with the topic.

- Do not expect to know or understand the employer's personnel policies or practices, so simply apply industry best practices or use the policies and practices of your current or most recent organization in your role playing.
- Do not make statements of what you can't say or do because of your lack of insight into how the employer does it there, that is unacceptable in a role play and minimizes your chances of demonstrating you are competent in the skill or ability being evaluated.

- Expect to be challenged over and over, because the scenario is often designed to evaluate how you respond to resistance and conflict from the other participant.

Presentation

The final interview style I cover in this book is the presentation. There are two types of presentations an employer may request during the recruitment process for a position. The first type is used to evaluate your presentation skills and the second type is used to learn your depth and breadth of subject matter expertise in a topic.

Employers use the presentation style of interviewing more heavily in life sciences, academic, sales and marketing, and consulting fields, where being in front of an audience is a critical factor in the success of the role for the company. The purpose is very different in the two styles of presentation interviewing and the observation and analysis is done differently for each.

When you are advised that an interview will involve a presentation, you will either be told to present a topic of your choice, or you will be provided a narrow range of topics acceptable to the organization. For example, if you are told that you are going to be given 10 minutes to present a topic of your choice during the interview using whatever media and delivery you wish, you can discern that the interview is focused on evaluating your ability to present to an audience. There is minimal concern by the employer of the topic, for all they care you can present on the history of cotton candy. The other type of presentation will involve the employer providing you a specific topic or category for which you are to present to the interviewer. In this case the employer is seeking to observe and evaluate the applicant's depth and breadth of knowledge on the subject they were directed to write about. When preparing for these interviews you want to recognize which style of presentation you are expected to deliver. When the topic is your choice, you should make every effort to present a topic relevant to the business of the employer you are presenting to. Understand that your delivery, communication, use of technology, and knowledge transfer to the audience are all key components of a successful presentation.

In contrast when given a specific topic, recognize there is an expectation that you will provide the audience depth and breadth of expert knowledge on the topic which will be relevant to the organization you are presenting to. An example of this would be a packaging engineer delivering information on a specific type of form fill seal product they developed to meet product specifications at a former employer. Another example would be an accountant walking through the entire year end close process to close the financials for a business unit.

Regardless of the type of presentation requested of you, be sure to ask the employer adequate questions to gain the information you need to be successful. Your questions should include length of presentation, ability to use technology for display, number of copies required if printed material is requested, who is in the audience, capabilities of the interview location for display, and how detailed they would like the topic to be.

Now that you have a clearer understanding of the interview styles and purpose of each used in industry, it is time to move into traditional and behavioral interview styles.

CHAPTER FIVE

TRADITIONAL INTERVIEW STYLE

Organizations will implement a variety of techniques to conduct and facilitate the interview process for applicant selection and ultimately for a hiring decision. Many organizations have developed a set of questions based on their existing job descriptions with emphasis on both the essential functions of the job, the additional skills, knowledge, and abilities needed to perform the role successfully, and questions that lend to discernment about culture fit with the business. In reality, what many of you will also experience is a plethora of questions by interviewers unrelated to the job, personal or inappropriate in nature and potentially non-compliant with federal, state, or local laws. The more informed an applicant you become the more effective you will be at taking some control from the employer during the interview process ensuring that you are treated fairly and appropriately during the process. Make the effort to review information provided at no cost by the U.S. Department of Labor Internet website with emphasis on regulatory enforcement agencies to include the Equal Employment

Opportunity Commission and the Office of Federal Contracts Compliance Programs. The insight you gain will position you to recognize when an employer is asking you questions that are illegal during the recruitment process or inappropriate at specific stages of the process. This chapter will not delve further into what types of questions are legal or illegal to ask during an interview, as this book is not focused on legislative compliance or training for a hiring manager. This book is about you, the applicant, and gaining strategic insight into the types of questions asked of applicants, and the purpose or goal of asking them.

We start with exploring the traditional interview questions you might be accustomed to or familiar with. The term traditional is simply an industry reference to questions asked during interview processes with a focus on cognitive ability, personality, and hypothetical situations. There is nothing wrong with traditional style questions, as there is a great deal to gain in the responses to these questions. The reason you are being presented with this information is to understand what is being asked of you as the applicant, and how best to prepare your responses so you articulate your capabilities and competence as efficiently and effectively as possible to achieve success.

A key strategy to execute during the interview process is to identify the type of question being asked, and leveraging your wisdom to respond in a manner that positions you for meeting the expectations and needs of the organization. Recognizing a question is in the traditional form will allow you to apply the techniques in this book to deliver a response unexpected by the interviewer and potentially unmatched by competing applicants.

A traditional question is often close ended and will focus on what you are capable of doing versus a demonstration of competence and experience performing a task or activity. Questions may be exploring who you are versus what skills you have. For example, you may be asked "Tell me about yourself?" in which case the response cannot in any way, shape, or form be related to an essential function of the position. Regardless, organizations have been asking this question of applicants for a very long time. Applicants need to be cautious about how they answer questions such as these, since they are not job related and unless you master the art of an elevator speech in which you encapsulate your competence and capabilities with your successes in sixty seconds or less, you could be sharing more than you want to with a potential employer. "Why do you want to work here?" is another question that is traditional and is unrelated to the essential functions of the position. However, for the employer, this question demonstrates enthusiasm and interest in the company and could reflect the level of research and effort the applicant exerted to learn about the opportunity for which they are interviewing for.

What you can certainly expect in some form or another is the traditional question of strengths and weaknesses. In a later chapter we explore in detail how to handle these questions, but recognize that these are used frequently for different reasons and the interviewer often attempts to limit the length of a response to a few words for each topic. Interviewers also may ask what type of goals you have during the interview, limiting the scope of the response to a certain time period. This is another example of a traditional question that is unrelated to the essential functions of the job but may be impactful to the employer based on what you say and the context of the response in relation to the position you are applying for.

Traditional questions related to cognitive abilities are focused on your ability to blend various basic cognitive skills to perform tasks in the workplace. The questions could range from simple questions such as "Can you read, write, and speak English?" or "Can you work a cash register?" A cognitive question will be seeking to understand how your basic brain activities are applied to tasks and activities in the workplace. The employer will be looking for a much higher level of capability in blending basic skills into complex tasks facing employees today, such as using computer and web based tools and technology to equipment and machinery that are automated. Most interviewers have been asking these traditional questions for so many years that the fundamental purpose of the questions are lost in relation to cognition and they only understand the question as common and appropriate for most situations.

A hypothetical traditional question may have been the forerunner of the more practical and effective style of behavioral interview commonly used today by organizations during the selection process. There is a significant difference in the execution and application of the question since the traditional method is to learn from an applicant what they "would" do if the situation presented itself to them in the workplace. For example, "What would you do if a customer became irate with you or a peer in the store?" This question can be easily handled by any applicant as you will learn in detail later in this book, and produces little to no evidence that the applicant could actually perform the task in a real situation. Every individual is capable of doing just about anything, with the right time, support, training, resources, and tools, etc. This question presented in a traditional format, which you might often encounter, provides the applicant a great opportunity to apply any and all knowledge they have to respond to the question since they are not being required to demonstrate or prove they have done the activity.

They say someone can be dangerous with a little bit of knowledge, well that is true and during an interview when asked what you would do the interviewer has opened the door to learn nothing about your experience or competence, but rather what you know you are capable of. This may be sufficient, but you will learn strategic responses to hypothetical questions and master methods to articulate your experience and competence when these questions are presented to you.

For a quick review of this topic, a traditional interview question is fundamentally a common interview question that may not be related to the essential functions of the job you applied for that solicit information an employer uses to determine your fit for their organization. Recognizing when a question is traditional with the goal of responding as if the question was behavioral is a technique you will gain as you read on.

CHAPTER SIX

BEHAVIORAL INTERVIEW STYLE

Now that you have a better understanding of the types of interviews and the traditional style of interviewing it is time to gain a deeper understanding of the behavioral interviewing style. When teaching individuals about behavioral interviewing I enjoy reminiscing about financial commercials of the 1980s. You may or may not have direct exposure to this reference, however it will be just as meaningful. Several of the financial investment and planning companies would advertise their products and services and conclude the commercial with that fast talking legal disclaimer. The specific disclaimer being referenced is "Past performance is not indicative of future results. Invest wisely." Sound familiar? Perhaps you have other similar references that might make the same point. In any case, this is a very accurate statement in the context of financial planning and investments. This book is not about financial investments, but it is about investing in yourself by gaining knowledge to improve your interviewing capabilities. Back to this statement and behavioral interviewing. Industrial and organizational psychologists and human resource professionals have gained insight over time allowing them to recognize that while this statement may be inaccurate for the financial world, there is prudent applicability regarding human capital. In other words, in the context of the workplace and dealing with people there may be value in this statement.

Specifically, consider the following statement that you will need to read a few times and digest to fully capture the point when it comes to interviewing practices and the workplace. Do not concern yourself with any other context outside of the workplace. "Work performance behaviors of the past are accurate predictors of future work performance in a similar situation."

What does this concept mean for you as an applicant during the interview process? Quite simply that when you are participating in an interview it is going to be critically important for you to not only provide static answers to interview questions, but articulate your responses in such a way that you demonstrate the past work performance experience giving evidence you can succeed in the tasks in the future.

Employers have been designing and developing behavioral interview questions for many years now. What appears to have been missed is the communication, training, and development of interviewing skills to appropriately and adequately respond to this style of interview by a large portion of the applicant population. The goal of this chapter is to provide you a broad understanding of the behavioral interviewing style and prepare you to better articulate your responses during an interview.

As a reminder, nothing in this text is designed to have you discount your knowledge, skills, abilities, and experience in your career thus far. Rather this text will teach you how to gain greater mastery in the articulation and communication of your experience and what you have to offer a potential employer. At the same time, you are gaining strategic exposure to the tactics and techniques of an employer during the recruitment process so you are better equipped and prepared for executing the process as an applicant more successfully.

Think about the traditional style of interviewing and the following question. "Have you ever dealt with a difficult or an irate customer?" This question, while important to the employer to know what experience you have regarding customer service and conflict management, fails to actually solicit the information necessary to make an informed decision about the applicant. Anyone receiving this question can simply respond "yes" and the question has been answered. Two terrible results emerge in this scenario due to the manner in which the question was asked. First, it is a closed ended question with no room for expanding on the response without further probing. Second, it limits the applicant's ability to tell the employer **how** they dealt with difficult or irate customers in the past. In my opinion, the latter is the greater mistake by using a traditional question to gather the information. Now we will contrast the interview question style by using a behavioral interview question to emphasize the points.

A behavioral question with the goal of learning about the applicant's experience with customer service could be "Provide a recent example of when you dealt with an irate customer and what the results of your efforts were." Is the difference clear to you? It may not be, which is why more explanation and additional examples are provided.

When presented with the behavioral questions in the interview, which may come across as a request more than a question, the applicant must demonstrate the skills the employer is looking for by using a recent work experience to respond. Taking this line of thought further, the applicant not only needs to tell the interviewer what happened, but they must detail **how** they performed the activities to handle the customer. This style of question can be very intimidating to an unprepared applicant, causing them to scramble for a response and fumble through the answer. At the same time what this book will teach you is that the behavioral style question is the most advantageous for you because it is open ended and allows you to take control of the process and demonstrate a wide range of experience and competence. When applying the techniques learned from this book you will also be improving your communication skills and demonstrating effectively in front of the employer your ability to articulate information. In a later chapter we will explore in greater detail the response process for this type of interview style question.

To solidify your understanding of the principles related to the behavioral interview, consider some additional examples of questions provided below. You are shown the topic, the traditional question you might be asked, and a behavioral question you might be asked to obtain evidence of expertise by the interviewer.

Topic	Traditional Style Question
	Behavioral Style Question
Effective Communication	**Do you have the ability or experience to influence others when communicating with them?**
	Describe how you have used your ability to influence others to solve a complex problem in the workplace.
Ability to Prioritize	**Do you prioritize your work?**
	Describe how you currently prioritize your work, and explain what you have done when priorities have changed.
Ethical Dilemma	**Have you ever faced an ethical dilemma in the work-place?**
	Provide a recent example of a workplace ethical dilemma you have experience and how you handle the situation.

In each of these examples the applicant must be prepared to understand the full context of the question and be competent enough to provide a comprehensive response that satisfies the real goal of the question. What you may begin to see is the true purpose of the question being asked during the interview. For example, when asked "Do you prioritize your work?" the answer is obviously yes. Who doesn't prioritize their work even if they do not realize they are doing it. We all prioritize, and the question and answer produce little to no information about the applicant for the employer to make an informed decision. Now consider the wording and goal of the behavioral example question above. The applicant is going to have do provide real life experience in prioritizing in response to the question that informs the interviewer about several skills and competencies of the applicant. The interviewer is seeking to not only determine if the applicant prioritizes their work, but they want recent examples of how they have done so. Taking it even further without a follow up probing question the interviewer is also going to obtain information about the applicant's experience or ability to adapt and shift priorities when business circumstances change. The response you provide the interviewer will solicit follow up questions in which the employer will learn even more about your expertise. Key note here is that the employer is asking this question for a reason, not just to learn about how you prioritize. Remember questions are supposed to be related to the essential functions of the role, therefore this question is being asked because the role you have applied for requires the successful incumbent to prioritize and potentially multi task and shift priorities frequently.

So what have you learned here? That not only will the question be more comprehensive giving you an opportunity to share more than in a response to a traditional question, but you will be gaining insight into the position if you break down the questions asked and relate them back to the requirements and responsibilities of the position.

What does that do for you in an interview setting? It creates an awareness that allows you to provide responses that not only answer the question, but presents and articulates your expertise in performing the task which is what the employer is looking to determine about you. Poor interview questions produce poor responses and create challenges in making hiring decisions. The more effective the question and the more comprehensive and articulate the response, the more successful an interview for both parties and a higher chance of success for you as the applicant.

Now earlier you learned that employers still use traditional questions during an interview. You also learned that this style of interview question is not the most effective for the employer or the applicant. Therefore the strategy I want you to implement during your interviews is a transition from a traditional response to a behavioral response, even if the question is not posed in that format. This is not as easy as it sounds, but with practice and preparation you will be able to turn each and every question presented to you into a comprehensive response that demonstrates your experience and competence in performing the task. Execute this strategy well and you will provide the interviewer insight into your workplace behaviors empowering the interviewer to make a more informed decision about your candidacy for the position you applied for.

CHAPTER SEVEN

PREPARATION –
THE APPLICATION

Completing a job application may be as simple as filling in some boxes on a printed document and handing it in to a manager at a business or as complicated as a complex ATS system with a profile, pages of data entry, and attaching files to complete the application process. No matter how brief or complicated the application process is, recognize that the employer determines the process and has an obligation to be consistent and fair to all applicants. This does not imply that some organizations do not bypass established practices and policies when it is convenient or advantageous for them to do so. The point here is that compliance demands a consistent and fair application process for all applicants and failure to adhere to this premise can create risk for their business.

Read all of the instructions provided by an employer's job posting or internet careers section to ensure you complete all steps of the process. Regulations allow for an employer to dictate their application process, and as noted above the employer simply needs to be consistent. Beyond this obligation, there is no significant guidance on what an employer may or may not require to be considered an applicant. When using an ATS, there is tremendous clarity on when an interested individual actually becomes an applicant. This transformation takes place once the ATS process is complete and submitted with all required attachments, and often requires electronic signature to finalize the application.

When the application instructions require additional documents, attachments, transcripts, or other materials, plan your submission carefully and make sure you organize all of the materials with appropriate file names retaining copies for yourself for later reference. Something as simple as failing to put the required job posting number in the subject line of an email or neglecting to attach an Equal Opportunity Employment form could negate your status as an applicant long before your qualifications are even considered.

A factor that some applicants do not think about is the cross referencing of an application to a resume by the employer. Don't for a minute think that you can bypass completing the application in a comprehensive and complete manner if the employer requires it to be completed by submitting your resume with it. This is a serious mistake many applicants make resulting in being disqualified and never knowing why. An employer wants to believe that you care about their organization, and that you are willing to take the time and put in the effort to complete their application. When you don't, hiring managers or human resource professionals can become biased towards your application and discount you for failing to comply with the application instructions. Do not leave job detail sections of an application blank or enter "see resume" when the application requests job information. You must do one of two things, highlight and summarize your current role, or include as much information as will fit in the space provided and then add additional pages to the application. The employer will appreciate the effort and will have more respect for you. Ultimately, the employer may review your resume knowing their application has limited space to explain what you did at your current or prior employer. However, and this is really important, there is no legal basis for an employer to review a resume. So when you don't complete their application and indicate "see resume", you may be disqualified and it would be a compliant action by the employer. Perhaps you never realized that the application itself was a critical component in the recruitment process, but as you are learning each step has a purpose and there are strategies to ensure you meet all of the expectations of the employer so you can secure the job interview.

While this guidance may be simplistic as well, it may be the most important for you as an applicant. Be honest and accurate in your application because if the employer determines you have been dishonest you may be disqualified as an applicant. This is known in industry as misrepresentation, the willful inclusion of false or inaccurate information on an application. Now this does not mean that when you said you worked from July 24 to November 15 and the reality is July 21 to November 12 that you will be disqualified, as we are all human and our memory and recollection is not always perfect. However, if you were never the supervisor and you list that you managed some of the staff, a reference check may demonstrate you misrepresented your experience and that is a direct reflection of your work ethic and morals creating a problem for the employer resulting in disqualification.

Appropriately handling compensation on an application is a question individuals have asked me about for years. Before I share my guidance to you on inclusion or exclusion of compensation on your application I want to share industry practices related to compensation data and perspective from twenty years of experience related to the use of compensation information on an application.

First I want you to think about a reference check for past employment. Most employment reference check companies, banks, mortgage brokers, and other financial organizations understand the current legislative climate with regards to privacy rights and the protection of personal information. In parallel human resources professionals are experienced and trained in appropriate handling of employee data and information. When you consider both of these factors you begin to realize it is extremely difficult, if not impossible for an employer to find out what your compensation is in your current or a previous role. In fact, ethical organizations do not permit anyone outside of human resources to handle employment and financial reference checks and require the requesting third party to provide a signed authorization by the employee before releasing any information. With the rise of employment litigation, caution and compliance have led organizations to establish clear practices or policies for the release of any data. For the most part an ethical company will only release (1) the employee's title; (2) dates of employment; and (3) confirm if currently employed. Only when specific authorization to release compensation will the employer provide such information to a third party.

The second concept I want you to consider is the reality that someone who is qualified for a position should not be treated unfairly based on the level of compensation previously earned. In other words, if you were earning $120,000 in your previous position and you are applying for a position that only pays $85,000, the employer should not discount your application based on the fact you previously earned a higher salary. This fallacy by employers was emphasized during the 1990s and 2000s when many large corporations experienced layoffs and downsizing, resulting in large reductions in force. When applying for jobs to care for their families many applicants were not afforded equal opportunity for positions they were qualified for simply because of their previous compensation. Just because someone earned more money in the past does not preclude them from accepting a position of lower compensation in the future. Employers have a regulatory obligation to avoid discrimination and to ensure a fair recruitment process. However, there is nothing that prohibits an employer from discriminating against someone because of how much compensation they earned in the past. Therefore, while there are strategies to aid with this part of the application, recognize that bias happens and there are organizations that will discount a qualified person simply because of the compensation they listed on their application.

This whole concept is about the view by an employer that someone is over qualified. In my experience there is no such thing as being over qualified. You are either qualified, or you are not. You may be more qualified than other applicants, and you may have more industry or professional experience compared to the normal demographics of applicants for the position. In either case if you meet the job requirements you are qualified. The rejection of your application is going to be made by a person reviewing the application. The reality is employers fear hiring someone who may not stay long with the organization, may not be a good culture fit, or the applicant may really be seeking a higher level position and will cause disruption to operations if hired. At the same time more organizations are realizing the value of experienced workers and are learning how to leverage their expertise through efforts in diversity and inclusion programs. At the end of the day if you are qualified and willing to accept the compensation being offered for the position you applied, you have every right to advance in the recruitment process.

Back to the guidance on what you should do on the application. Unless you are concerned about sharing your compensation, include it and be honest and accurate. However applications rarely if ever give you an opportunity to reflect total compensation. Total compensation is the total value of all the wages/salary earned in addition to benefits provided. For example, if you earn $50,000, receive company match on your medical, dental and vision premiums, have matching contributions to a 401(k), and receive paid time off of 3 weeks, your total compensation may actually be very different than the $50,000 you indicate on the application, and be more like $62,000 annually. So when it comes time to discuss an offer and compensation, think clearly about what your total compensation was versus just wages or salary alone.

Most ATS applications will not ask you to enter a compensation value and instead now offer you a range to select. What you want to focus on is not the selection for your current or past compensation, but there is almost always a question about how much are you seeking to make. This question is important to align with the job posting if the compensation was posted. The ATS may use your response to include or reject your application because an employer established criteria for all applicants. Compensation questions are complicated and can create obstacles and challenges in the application process. Focus on making sure you complete all requirements of the application and put less emphasis on your past compensation.

When completing an application, you are often required to provide work experience sequentially. List your current or most recent position first, and then work sequentially backwards. If you happen to work multiple jobs during the same time period list them both, do not add second jobs at the end of the application, it becomes confusing to the employer.

Read and review your application before submission, either in paper format or electronically when the ATS offers you to preview the application. Avoid typographical or grammatical errors on the application, as just about every job has the requirement of "good written and oral communication skills" and therefore when there are mistakes on the application it reflects failure in meeting one of the job requirements or expectations of the position.

In the current legislative climate of affirmative action and equal opportunity employment as well as recent executive orders that increase regulatory reporting for employers, you will find yourself facing in paper or electronic format a questionnaire about your race, ethnicity, veteran status, and disability status. There are strict regulations about what can be asked and when, and at all times you must be advised in writing that providing the information is completely optional and does not impact your application. Be comfortable and confident with providing this information, because as noted in a prior chapter, ATS are designed to separate and hide this information from the recruiting process and is only used for reporting purposes. When in paper format, there is no guarantee that bias is not taking place, however the human resource profession prides itself on conducting business in an ethical manner. Over the years I have heard stories of applicants listing themselves as minorities or female thinking that gave them an advantage in the recruitment process. It does not, and as far as reporting is concerned a workforce representation of gender and race of actual employees is reported as well as the applicant tracking reports and comparisons are made for determination of adverse or disparate impact in personnel activities.

To summarize this chapter, applications are a critical component of the recruitment process. The employer dictates the process and as an applicant you must comply or risk rejection. Be sure you provide accurate and honest information, be sequential with work experience, and ensure your application matches your resume if you plan to include or provide a resume later in the process.

CHAPTER EIGHT

PREPARATION – THE RESUME

This is the chapter in which we dispel myths and legends about resumes. I have been interacting with applicants for over 20 years and it never ceases to amaze me how some recruiting or human resource professionals, and perhaps business managers, have tainted the purpose and use of a resume. Individuals are led to believe that the prettier the resume is, the nicer the formatting, and the thicker the bond paper the more value the resume creates. Applicants have also been led to believe that a resume should not be more than two pages in length. Why are these views promulgated and how in the world do they ever sustain momentum? In communicating with peers in the human capital field during my career never have I been told, taught, or advised on the required or maximum length of a resume. In fact, with the modern advances in technology and the use of video resumes, online applications, social media, and other mediums of communication it is surprising to me that this view continues to manifest itself each and every time I teach applicants successful strategies and techniques to use in their resume.

Take a moment to reflect on the concept of the resume. An applicant is expected to complete an application, often being required to list up to ten years of work experience. Now translate that into a resume in which you are detailing your work experience, knowledge, skills, abilities, and competencies in one organized and succinct document. Would you expect someone with ten to fifteen or more years of experience to fit all relevant and critical information on just two pages? Having recruited for many years for a variety of industries I can tell you that there is no minimum or maximum requirement associated with a resume.

This does not mean that there are not recruiters, human resource professionals, and business managers that would enjoy their job much more if they didn't have to read long boring resumes during the recruitment process, especially when the resume is poorly written or filled with buzz words and information that fails to demonstrate or articulate the experience and competence of the applicant. It is understandable that over time when a recruiter at a Fortune 500 company may have to fill 20 positions a month and review 2,000 resumes submitted into their ATS that shorter would be more convenient, but that is not the goal of the resume. If you really reflect on this topic, think about the profile and application you complete in a comprehensive ATS. There may be six or seven sections of data you enter to build and create the application. Certainly to then make the statement that a resume should be two pages or less would be ridiculous and illogical.

Regarding the length of the resume, the strategy is to make sure you follow the following insight when writing your resume so that it is not filled with nonsensical information that fails to communicate and articulate who you are and what your experience and competence is as a potential employee.

Before we dive deeper into the important topic of the resume, I want to ensure you have clarity on the difference between a resume and a curriculum vitae (CV). For the vast majority of industries and professions, a resume will be used as the supplemental document to an application. However there will be employers that request a CV instead of a resume. These organizations will either be international businesses for which a CV is a more common term to represent in writing work and academic experience, or the organization will be in the life sciences or academic field. There is a reason for using a CV, and it stems from the presentation of work product by the applicant compared to work experience. A CV generally includes academic information in detail, and then all publications, presentations, authorships, research projects, fellowships, and so on. In recent years I have reviewed a few CVs that were over 25 pages in length detailing every publication and article the individual ever contributed to or authored themselves. This book is not going to cover the development or techniques for a CV since the mainstream of job applicants will be requested to or desire to have a resume representing their work experience.

As discussed in Chapter 3 you will ultimately want to have a text only version of your resume for use in ATS submissions, and it is highly recommended that you spend more time on the content of the resume than the formatting until it is written. Quite frequently the glaring problems with a resume are not just the typographical errors, but formatting errors because the applicant was attempting to get fancy with the document. The more complicated you attempt to get the greater the risk of error reflecting poor written communication skills during the recruitment process.

What is a resume supposed to be? It is an accurate documented reflection of your work experience and academic accomplishments. Around this core of information you might choose to include a professional summary or overview, or perhaps you prefer an objective. Somewhere in the resume you might decide to include a list of technical skills, soft skills, software applications and hardware used, and you may go as far as to list a section of accomplishments. Some applicants then include a list of references. The average resume will have all of these components and the strategies and techniques that follow will help you in designing and documenting your work experience and competencies efficiently, effectively, and in a manner that allows the recruiter, human resource professional, or business manager to easily distinguish your fit for their vacant position.

Here is what a resume is not, a job description. When you review job postings and vacancy information published by an employer you might note there are some common sections to the job posting. A job posting is not the same as a job description, but there are key elements of a job posting generally taken from the job description. The job posting informs an applicant of a vacancy, lists general or specific information about the vacant position, location, compensation, benefits, and other factors to attract an applicant to apply. A job description is a formalized document the employer maintains for a variety of purposes that is developed to explain why the position exists, what the essential functions of the role are, the knowledge, skills, abilities, and other characteristics (KSAOs) necessary to perform the duties of the position, and job requirements. In other words, a job description describes what an incumbent in the role is supposed to do. Allow that last sentence to sit with you for a moment. What a person is supposed to do in the position, not what the individual in the position actual did do or how they did it. This is where, in my opinion, the greatest mistake is made in the design and development of a resume. An applicant will list bullets or a paragraph of all the job description items for the position they held implying that it describes their work experience. It does not, and instead, for the trained recruiter, human resource professional, or business manager, it becomes crystal clear that the applicant only presented what they were supposed to do but nothing about their actual experience and competency doing the tasks. This can be a major flaw as you will learn here both in the resume and in the articulation of your experience in the job interview. There is nothing wrong with using paragraph style or bulleted lists to present your information, it is more about personal preference. From the perspective of a recruiter, I would rather see a brief summary of 1-2 sentences about the position and then a bulleted list representing the various work experiences and accomplishments during the tenure of that position.

A fallacy in the development of a resume includes not only listing your experience as a job description, but failing to articulate your actual expertise and how you performed the work, as well as what you accomplished. For this I want to teach you what I have shared with thousands of applicants and managers alike in both preparing a resume and reviewing a resume. Your goal for each position must be to relate your experience in understanding the tasks and responsibility, taking action to execute the tasks and responsibility, and articulate what the end result was. The strategy to do this is something I call SAR – Situation, Action, Results. Note immediately that this is going to take more thought and care in communicating your work experience, but it is more than worth it when you have the final work product ready for submission to that next potential employer.

When you write your work experience, understand that not every single bullet will be in the format of SAR, it just isn't practical or realistic for each task or activity an individual performs. However, the majority of your resume should present your experience in this format to maximize your chance of impressing the resume reviewer with your ability to document, articulate, and present your work experience that will be ore applicable to the employer than a review of job description bullets.

Here are a few examples to stimulate those brain waves that are bursting with energy right now.

Job Description Bullets in Resume
- Responsible for supervising five people.
- Responsible for delivering high level of customer service.
- Excellent communication skills.
- Work in a fast paced environment.
- Effectively support project team.
- Design and implement reports and systems.

For some, this might be a nice list representing work experience by an applicant. Do you agree? At this point you should not agree, instead consider what you have learned about this job applicant based on the above bulleted information. What the resume reviewer for the employer learned about this applicants work experience was absolutely nothing. What they did gather was a list of things the incumbent in the role is supposed to do or perform. Really ponder this insight for a moment. I am going to break it down further to demonstrate why representing your work experience like a job description or without context and articulation of how you executed the work is a discredit to you and will hinder your ability to advance in the recruitment process. Before I present SAR representations and examples for the same six bullets of information, I am going to break down this important concept further one at a time.

In the first bullet, you would learn that the applicant was responsible for supervising five people. What you do not know is a host of factors and how or what the applicant actually did. If this is from the job description, the first gap in information is whether or not this position actually had five employees on this incumbents team. Perhaps it is the maximum or anticipated number of staff members, but in reality there were only one or two actually working for this role at the time. Big difference already, right? Just because an individual is responsible for something does not mean they executed the responsibility well. Did this applicant have high turnover due to poor management or leadership? Did the incumbent inherit the staff or were they involved in recruiting and hiring when there was a vacancy or growth required? How well did the supervisor develop and grow the staff, and is there any evidence the supervisory skills were effective in building a strong team? The answer to all of these questions is no, leaving a large gap in information that a well written resume could fill in if articulated well.

Same bullet item, what about the type of employees this supervisor was responsible for? Would it make a difference if the person supervised 5 summer interns versus the supervision of 5 middle managers? What about the type of employee, blue collar versus white collar, FLSA Exempt versus Non-Exempt, Union versus Non-Union? Are you beginning to think about the resume and your experience differently? Do you realize now that a few more details and a lot less job description can be the difference between stating on a resume what you are supposed to do versus what you did? More insight is just ahead.

Bullet two is about customer service and the delivery of such at a high level. What does this mean? You are on the top of a mountain when you deliver customer services, or perhaps you are standing on the top of a desk when dealing with customers. Not at all, but if you consider this is written like a job description, of course an employer wants to convey the need to deliver a high level of service. It is really about the quality of the services being provided, not the height, right? Again you can note that we learn nothing about the applicant's experience in performing or delivering customer services. We don't even know who the customers are and if they are remote or in person, are they internal or external, and if the performance of this task utilized any technology such as telephone, internet chat, email, etc.

The third bullet is very humorous to read from the employer side, because the applicant would like to imply they have excellent communication skills, and yet as you can see from the first two bullets they failed to articulate just about anything specific about their work experience. I would say at this point they are fair at best in communication. I am not sure I have ever met a business leader or hiring manager that was looking for an applicant with poor communication skills. This is a given, however how you address and articulate this skill through the resume is an art. There is nothing being shared in this book that will lead an applicant to fabricate or misrepresent their work experience. What this information will enlighten you to do is think about who you are and your work experience from a different context and perspective, SAR. A few examples of what is missing here is who the incumbent primarily communicates with, what type of information was communicated, such as general or technical information, what medium was used to communicate, and what was effected by the communication to meet the goals and objectives of the business.

In the fourth bullet we see the attempt being made by the applicant to convey their ability to multi task or deal with high volume activities, but that is not what is written. What is also missing is how they accomplished their duties while working in a fact paced environment. Very little information if any about the applicant is communicated, and these are buzz words just about anyone can find on the internet to add or include on a resume that in reality have very little value for the employer without more context.

The next bullet is about supporting a project team and there is minimal context about how it was done or who the team is. A team leader or supervisor may make the mistake of using this bullet to represent how they led a team, by supporting them. This is true in the sense of providing an employee the tools, resources, and support they need to be successful, but the first bullet is where this experience should be captured. We do not know what this effectively correlates to in practicality, and the size of the team and or hierarchical level of the team is unclear. This information doesn't allow the recruiter to discern if this applicant was the team gopher or their subject matter expert with an integral role in the organization's success. Is the strategy and technique becoming clearer as you read these examples?

The word design is very effective and widely used in a resume. In this case it starts the job description bullet and then informs the reader of nothing more than what the incumbent is responsible for. This particular item should actually be the most comprehensive and in the form of SAR. You can leverage this item to communicate the technologies used to develop or communicate reports, and the system designed to gather, analyze, and compile the information used in the reports. The recipients of the report is also key to informing the resume reviewer of the audience the report is prepared for, and whether the information if technical in nature would add context. It would also be prudent to include the frequency of the report generation, and dependencies and stakeholders of the report, and the end use and value of the report.

Now that your head is spinning with ideas about your own work experience and resume, with a plethora of changes and improvements you can make, let us look at the same six bullets of information written more effectively to articulate experience and competence in the SAR structured format.

Work Experience in SAR Format in Resume
- Directly supervised and managed five senior accounting professionals by establishing performance goals, monitoring productivity and performance, communication of regular constructive feedback, and the

execution of accountability measures to ensure the achievement of business objectives and individual professional development. Several staff have received promotions during my time leading them.

• Demonstrated high level of customer service to the public in this retail location through active listening, modeling appropriate mannerisms, accepting diversity of thought, staying informed of current trends, and managing conflict with disappointed or irate customers resulting in several recognition awards and repeat sales.

• Successfully minimized barriers between functional units of the organization by demonstrating various communication techniques ranging from active listening to collaboration and influence in order to achieve unprecedented stakeholder support for launching a new procedure resulting in efficiency and cost savings of over $250,000 for the organization.

• Improved efficiency of call center productivity 20% by training staff on techniques to multi task through prioritization of the inbound calls into a call queue and the development of a web based knowledge system with frequently asked questions and template forms.

• Worked with a cross functional team of subject matter experts to facilitate the coordination of meetings, calendars, and travel. Created project materials in Microsoft Word, Excel, and PowerPoint to effectively communicate and distribute reports and information on time and within budget. Competent execution of these responsibilities enabled the project to be completed as scheduled and to meet the expectations of the internal stakeholders and external customers.

- Upon entering the role identified numerous gaps in the workflow, use of technology, and delivery of products to the customer. Designed and implemented new process workflow mapping to alleviate identified bottlenecks in our processes, reallocated resources where they could be most effective, and established metrics to measure progress to goals and track job performance and work productivity using Microsoft Visio, Project, and an integration software to communicate the information to our enterprise resource planning tools. This project was extremely impactful on our bottom line profits by impacting cost of making goods, resource allocation and planning, and use of technology to forecast future deliverables.

Is it easy to see the contrast between the two styles of writing a resume? There is nothing fabricating or misrepresented in the SAR format, rather the actual work performed by the applicant is detailed and explained in a much more comprehensive manner without buzz words and with clear purpose and results. These items in a resume inform the reader of the situation, the action taken by the applicant, and the results of the efforts. When you craft your resume in this manner you will quickly realize you do not need a section labeled accomplishments because you will master embedding the accomplishments as the results of each item you add to your resume. The most effective type of professional I have observed with using this style of writing a resume is a salesperson. If you ever read the resume of a salesperson, it is covered with quotas, sales results, rankings, year to year percentages and comparisons, etc. Why does a salesperson include all of this data and information versus simply stating they sold products or services? Because it would tell the reviewer nothing, and instead they have mastered SAR and learned to provide valuable information to their audience. In the same manner you must realize the resume may be that one document you are relying on to sell yourself to an employer, and if there is ever a time when you do not want to sell yourself short it is in a resume. Therefore, avoid like the plague writing a resume that looks like a job description and revise what you have into the SAR style which will empower you to really present your work experience and competencies.

Earlier we mentioned a section of the resume you may choose to include is a summary or objective. Be very mindful of which you select and how you maintain it as current or accurate for the position you apply for. If you are an active job seeker and you are submitting your resume ten, twenty, or a hundred different places online, you will be damaging your credibility and chances of an interview if your objective does not match the position you applied for.

This practice is not uncommon but will open the door for reviewer bias not because of typographical or grammatical error but as a result of carelessness and lack of effort to ensure the resume is appropriately written for the job you applied for. Believe it or not each employer wants to feel like they are the best employer and that you really want nothing more than to work for them. Hence, when you submit your application and resume for that dream engineering manager position and your resume objective indicates you are looking for a contract engineering opportunity you will be sending the wrong message indeed. Therefore, take time if you create an objective section to update or edit it for each submission confirming it is applicable to the role you applied for. I generally direct applicants away from using an objective and instead recommend using a summary.

The summary is only two to three sentences that at a very high level describe who you are and what experience you have. This would be similar to the development of an elevator speech which is brief and to the point yet conveys as much information as possible to your audience.

Are you beginning to see the wide spectrum of information, details, and critical nature of a resume and how a trained professional will review and dissect the information you provide? Unless you have experience reviewing resumes, sitting in the interview, making hiring decisions, and ultimately have had to terminate a bad hire it is difficult to grasp the complexity and importance of the resume. When we move into later chapters on the strategies during the actual interview, this will tie together nicely as you will understand how you must be able to demonstrate and prove in the interview what you wrote on the resume.

When listing your work experience, be sure to sequence the information by date in reverse order starting with your current or most recent position. It is much more effective to list each employer, and then the various titles or positions you held while with that organization. This allows you to demonstrate loyalty to the employer while also showcasing movement in the company such as to different functional areas or promotions resulting in greater responsibility. Key strategy for you as an applicant in writing the resume is to not only sequence effectively, but you must avoid duplication and demonstrate increased mastery over time. What does this mean for you? Earlier we dismissed the myths about the length of a resume, however applicants still worry about how long their resume is when all is said and done. If space on the resume is so valuable do not waste it by repeating your experience over and over or including items that really are unnecessary and fail to inform the audience of what is important. I know, another example will help bring this strategy into clarity.

For this example we will make the assumption that the applicant is presently a retail store manager for any large retailer such as Walmart or Target. Here is a list of the titles the applicant has held during their tenure at the retailer: Greeter, stock room assistant, sports department service worker, cashier, team leader, inventory manager, assistant store manager, and store manager. Now think about what duties each of these positions might perform as the individual advanced their career and gain new skills and experience.

On this applicant's resume would you expect to see under the section for store manager "placing products on shelves and properly labeling them" or "use of a cash register to accept payment for products and provide customer change"? Hopefully your response was no, as these experiences and competencies were mastered in earlier positions in their applicant's career. The goal when articulating who you are and your experience is to show progressive experience with increasing responsibility. This means that when you look at your current resume, do you see any experience, skills, or perhaps job description bullets that you have repeated from past jobs into more recent positions? If so, modify and change them so that you utilize the space on the resume to present unique and informative information in each and every job. Recognize that the hiring manager, recruiter, or human resource professional has training and experience to understand progressive skills and experience. If someone stocked shelves and then managed a cash register ten years ago and is now a manager of people who perform those duties it is unlikely that the individual needs to highlight today on an interview for a management level position their ability to perform those tasks, it is simply understood they know how to do it.

In the same fashion, those positions from early in your career should be used to present foundation and fundamental skills and expertise that you have built upon as you advanced in your career. Each sequential position should demonstrate in SAR style an increase in depth or breadth of KSAOs and the competency you have mastered through this point in your career.

Exploring another aspect of the development of a resume leads us to documenting gaps in employment. Many applicants fear revealing a time when they were unemployed or a stay at home parent, or a caregiver for a family member in which a gap in employment history will be reflected on their resume. Here is the facts about gaps in employment, they are okay, they happen, and we are all human and experience the obstacles and challenges in life that lead us on our way. The strategy I offer you related to gaps in employment is to document them and put the information in front of the employer rather than hide it. Here is why, and the bigger picture behind the guidance.

It is better to be honest and present the information affirmatively than to exclude the information and cause the gap to become a catalyst for further unnecessary inquiry that distracts from the rest of the resume or even the rest of an interview. The employer can either view the honest representation of your career and gaps in employment as credibility and sound ethics or they can discount your application based on your experience and background reflecting inadequate information to meet the job requirements. However, listing the gaps does not negatively impact the skills you do have, and therefore if you take the advice in this book I am providing you and develop a SAR style resume, the gaps will be ignored as human blips in your life that took you away from what you normally do professionally. At the same time, be strategic in how you articulate the absence. For example, don't present a gap as laid off and living off of a severance payment. Just list unemployed seeking employment. If you were a stay at home parent, simply list homemaker or caregiver. If you were attending classes and going to school to increase your knowledge and skills, indicate attending school during the gap. Regardless of the reason, try to minimize or eliminate any gaps in employment history, because during an interview, anything not present in the resume will raise concerns for the interviewer and that means time will be spent discussing the gap versus your experience, competency, and fit for their organization.

I have stated this before and will reiterate again, the individuals who are tasked with reviewing your resume are human, and as such hold, develop, or demonstrate bias in their review and selection process even if it is subconsciously. In my two decades of involvement with leading and managing recruitment life cycles, I have encountered some of the most unusual biases towards applicants that often could not be explained. Sometimes it was the name of the applicant, sometimes the email address being unprofessional. Other times it was the home address in a bad neighborhood, or a certain college the applicant went to. No matter what the reason, bias exists and what I am going to challenge you to do is eliminate as many potential indicators that lead to bias as possible from your resume. So how do you protect yourself from this bias as well as potential discrimination?

Be cautious when listing anything unrelated to work experience, such as memberships, associations, clubs, and organizations. While there is value in the information and you should be commended for all you do, it only takes one resume reviewer to not like the church group you belong to, have something against the girl scouts, or dislike the organization you are a member of to reject your resume and you will never know why. I do not recommend to applicants removing these items specifically, but I do advise to be selective in what you share and to find alternative methods of informing the audience of the resume your involvement in these activities. Here is the best approach to use on the resume. Instead of listing specific organization names list your role/title such as "volunteer" and indicate you are actively involved in volunteering with local organizations that aid and serve the community. Since questions about these activities would most likely not be job related, you should not be asked about them during an interview. Using this strategy on the resume actually expands what you might be doing and represents the point you are trying to make, which is you are an active member of our society and volunteer your time to help others.

Age discrimination is a major problem that has been cause for regulatory action and legislation. I have firsthand experience with hiring managers discounting a resume simply because the applicant attended school or worked years before the hiring manager was even born. With the working population demographics constantly expanding and older workers finding the need to continue working past retirement age for financial or personal reasons, employers are faced with the risk and liability of an age discrimination law suit if they fail to properly train and monitor their recruitment practices. With that said, discrimination is often done individually and not systemically across an enterprise. The strategy for your resume is to document your work experience and education in such a way that you are doing your best to not reveal your approximate age. How do you accomplish this mighty task?

First, do not include dates with your educational experience on a resume if you believe it will expose you to discrimination. If you are actively attending school then list "currently in progress" so the employer knows you are a lifelong learner. However, for those of you thinking that you just can't leave off the dates, I ask you why not? Have you ever in your entire life reviewed a job posting that stated the following?

Job Requirements
- Bachelor of Science Degree in Finance from 1992-1994
- Cost Accounting practices from 2001
- Accounts Payable ability from 2004

You certainly shouldn't have, and most likely never will. But why? Because the job requirements including KSAOs, experience, and education only indicate what you must have, not when you obtained it. Pause and digest this information as it is very important concept to consume and shift your paradigm on this topic. If a position required a Bachelor Degree, then as long as you actually have earned a Bachelor Degree, you list it on your resume. I would do so with the name of the school, the type of degree, the major of the degree, and a GPA if you wish.

If an employer chooses to discuss the degree with you during an interview, then your application and resume was already successful in getting you to that stage in the process, which should reflect you are at least minimally qualified for the position. At that point the date of the degree should not matter, and the only time it may come up is during the pre-employment background check if performed to verify education.

Parallel to education documented on the resume, you want to be strategic with how much job history to list for the same reason of exposing your age to the employer. If you consider earlier guidance about increased mastery over time in the sequencing of your work experience, you will also recognize that your first job as a cashier at the convenience store or your waiter or waitress job during college are really irrelevant to the KSAOs and experience you need for the job for which you applied. Therefore the guidance for the resume is to stop listing full job details and experience after you go back about ten years, or adequately to represent the experience you need to demonstrate to the employer for the position you applied to. After the detailed section, include another section labeled "Prior Work Experience" and only include the company name and your title when you were employed there. This information may become a topic of discussion in the interview, but if you have a well written resume reflecting the other work experience you will nullify this information as a catalyst for discussion or concern.

Now a bit of advice on listing references on a resume. Do not do it! If the application required it, then do as it requests or risk rejection. If an ATS requests the information, same principles apply. However, a resume is your document that represents who you are and what experience you have. Therefore, there is no need to give the potential employer other leads to work on for filling their open positions. You also want to have an element to the resume that forces communication and interaction if they want the information. Therefore, simply include on a resume "References Available Upon Request" and leave it at that. Either the employer will be capturing the information from the application, during the interview process, or will not worry about it until after a contingent offer is made and they are performing the background check process. These reasons are enough for you to recognize there is no purpose in listing the references, yet I want to share another from a recruiting perspective just to demonstrate the value of a resume.

A recruiter will use any resume to gather a tremendous amount of information and a competitive advantage over other firms or recruiters who do not have the resume. I will list some of the uses for you to think about and consider and then wrap this chapter up with a summary.

- Email address – solicit other information from you
- Phone number – solicit other information from you
- Company names on resume – other sources of qualified applicants with similar skill sets as the applicant. For example, if you are an engineer it is likely you have worked for engineering companies, and therefore if I review your resume I will learn about other sources of applicant pools of individuals who are also in the engineering field

- Academic Institutions – gather intelligence on the types of schools that produce an engineer similar to the applicant for sourcing purposes and for resume searches
- References – excellent source of other contacts, other viable candidates for the same or other positions, and links to other organizations

As you can see a resume is a valuable source of information when used strategically by a well-trained individual. To summarize this chapter consider again these points.

- There is no minimum or maximum length for a resume
- There is a difference between a resume and a CV
- Focus your resume as SAR – Situation, Action, Results
- Do not write your resume as if it was a job description
- Sequence your experience and demonstrate increased mastery
- Document gaps in employment
- The summary or objective must be applicable
- Be cautious including memberships, clubs, and associations
- Do not include dates of education
- Do not list references
- **DO NOT MISREPRESENT!**

CHAPTER NINE

PREPARATION –
BEFORE THE INTERVIEW

The day is about to arrive as you have been scheduled for an interview onsite with the employer face to face. Do you just show up and hope it goes well? Of course not, and this book has already provided you with a wealth of strategies and information to change your outlook on the recruitment process. Now we enter the planning and preparation stage in which you will practice information you will learn in Chapter 10 and Chapter 11. But there is more you need to do than practice for the actual interview if you truly want to be prepared.

Learn everything you can about the employer, from recent news and events to members of the executive management team. Find out if possible the vision and mission of the organization and read what other people have to say about working for the organization or being a customer of the company. You want to be able to prepare questions for the interviewer(s) and demonstrate your enthusiasm, excitement, and desire to work for this employer. Conducting research that you can share during the interview will be beneficial to you in gaining a clearer picture of who you are seeking to work for and to the company who will value the effort you put into learning about them. Reach out to your network of friends, family, peers, and anyone else who may have insight into the inner workings of the business so you are better informed and prepared to anticipate and respond to questions asked of you during the interview.

Take time to review the job posting and any job description you may have been provided. There are two reasons for this: (1) you want to ensure you plan your responses that are certain to be asked related to the essential functions of the position; and (2) you want to be informed as to the scope of the role so if during the interview questions appear to be misaligned, you can counter the questions and ask about their relevance to the position you applied for.

While this advice may not be something you have never heard before, it is very important to plan ahead for traffic and other potential obstacles to arriving for the interview 10 minutes early. Using a global positioning system may not always be as effective as you would like, especially in more rural settings, so it is appropriate to test drive to the interview location to make sure you find the building where the interview is being held. Understand that from an employer's perspective punctuality for the interview is a reflection on your work ethic and what can be expected from your performance in arriving to work on time each day. A tardy arrival for an interview may result in cancellation of the interview, rejection, and a difficult conversation explaining why you were late.

Note that if there is a major challenge to arrival such as a highway being shut down due to an accident or unsafe travel conditions such as snow and ice, you should contact the employer and notify them you will be late as soon as you know you will be, and ask to reschedule if you cannot make it or apologize for the delay and communicate when you believe you will arrive. Employers deal with this type of situation every day with accidents and weather that are out of the employee's control hindering their arrival at work. As long as you are respectful and communicate effectively and timely you should be in a good position to continue in the process.

For many interviews the employer will request you bring a copy of your resume, references, performance reviews, or other work examples and documentation to the interview. From a preparation perspective make sure to have an adequate number of copies for each person you are scheduled to meet with. If the employer indicates you are meeting two people and you make two copies, and once you arrive you end up meeting four people, do not be so concerned since they did not inform you of the potential change. However to safeguard against this always have a few extra copies with you in the event you need them.

In most interviews there will be a time that you will be offered an opportunity to ask any questions you might have for the interviewer(s). Even if everything you think you wanted to know about the organization and position had been explained to you, never state that you have no questions for the company. That demonstrates a lack of interest in the role, organization, and individuals interviewing you. Further, early on I explained that an interview is two directional, meaning you should be attempting to gather as much information about the employer and the position to make an informed decision as the employer is gathering about you. So if at some point during the interview you are offered the opportunity to ask questions, you want to be prepared with questions.

I will not only guide you on asking questions but I will actually provide you a number of example questions you should be thinking about and asking during an interview. If you are interviewing with a single individual you may ask the questions a certain way compared to a panel interview in which you want to ask each member of the panel a different question. The purpose of prepared questions, in additional to gaining insight, is to turn the interview at this stage into a conversation if in the unfortunate event the interview had been all question and answer. These questions are to both develop a rapport with the interviewer(s), demonstrate your interest in the company and position, and open the door for additional questions by you for the employer. Mix and match them, use some or all of them, or develop your own as these are simple examples to promote your thinking about interaction with the employer.

- What happened to the former incumbent in this role?
- How long has the position been vacant?
- What do you believe is the greatest challenge for an individual to be successful in this role?
- Can you please describe for me the company culture?
- How long have you been with the company and why do you stay?
- What does management do to ensure engagement with the workforce?
- Are there systems in place to afford me the opportunity for professional development?

- What do you see as the current challenges facing this business today and how is the organization preparing to overcome those challenges?

There are, of course, questions to avoid during the interview which can mislead the interviewer into making assumptions or judgments about you that would most likely be inaccurate. Some of the following questions are valid and important, but should be asked after an offer is made. Prior to receiving an offer, these topics are moot because you do not want to be too excited and plan on what is to come until it is a reality. Do not set yourself up for a letdown, and therefore avoid asking these questions during the interview. Some of these questions are simply wrong to ask because they imply meanings that you should not want to express. By doing so you diminish any confidence the interviewer has in you being qualified or you reveal a lack of confidence which could damage your credibility.

- Is the work schedule flexible?
- Is overtime required?
- What experience are you looking for in an applicant?
- How many other applicants are there?
- How many people are you interviewing?
- If I am not selected for the position, will you be contacting me to let me know where I fell short?

These questions either have no value to you as an applicant, or simply are inappropriate to ask during the interview because they could reflect your desire to not meet the employer's expectations of the role. A significant amount of individuals have asked me why they should not ask about other applicants, those in total or those being interviewed. My response has not waivered, as there is no value in the information you gain from the response. For example, if you are told there were 1,000 other applicants and you are 1 of 10 being interviewed, how do you feel, better? What if they tell you there were only 8 applicants and they are interviewing all 8, how does that make you feel? I know psychologically you would like to believe the information results in some change in your mindset of your chances in getting the position, but I disagree. I could interview 10 people out of 1,000 and not hire any of them, or I could interview 8 out of 8 and decide to hire them all. Since the employer will withhold information as to how you might have ranked compared to others, and you need to enter the interview process with the confidence that the position is yours (assuming you are qualified), then there is really no purpose or value in wasting a question on a topic that can produce no positive results for you.

In a similar fashion, there is a time and place to ask the human resource questions. Waiting until you have the offer is acceptable for proposing your human resource questions related to compensation, benefits, paid time off, vacation or sick time, retirement and pension programs, voluntary benefits, pre-tax plans, deferred compensation, and any other information related to the total compensation for the position. If you ask about these items before the offer you again may be creating excitement before it is appropriate to do so. Besides, the position is generally posted with some information about the compensation and benefits, and the employer's website is often a valuable resource to gain this information.

Now you have some clarity on the types of questions you want to prepare for the employer. The last piece of advice in preparation before the interview is your attire. I have never claimed to be a fashion connoisseur and I never read or received training and any requirements for applicants, but I do know some of the do's and don'ts of interview attire.

First and foremost, and this may sound humorous, but whatever you decide to wear try it several days prior to the date of the interview. There is nothing like pulling up your pants and forgetting that last time you wore the suit the button broke off. Or perhaps you cannot get the blouse or shirt around your body to button, and your suit jacket has that stain from the holiday party you forgot about. The point is preparation and planning is a critical factor in your overall interview success. You want to ensure you adequate time to handle any obstacle thrown your way that could hinder your performance during the interview. One suggestion is for you to visit the employer's office or location and observe what the dress code is and what people are wearing. There is nothing in this century like showing up in a three piece suit for an interview with owners who are half your age wearing shorts and sandals, so you want to gain information from whomever scheduled your interview as to what is appropriate attire. You don't have to match the employer, but you want to be professional and somewhat aligned with the expectations of the organization. Females should wear either a skirt or a suit, males should wear a suit and tie, or pants, shirt and tie. Things to avoid are torn or damaged clothing, soiled clothing, miniskirts, tops that reveal midriff, low cut blouses that are inappropriately revealing, hats, sun glasses, or excessive jewelry. Any religious clothing is completely acceptable at all times.

Now we have wrapped up various aspects of planning steps for delivering the best interview of your life. Next I begin addressing the interview itself and strategies to execute during and after the interview.

CHAPTER TEN

PREPARING FOR COMMON INTERVIEW QUESTION THEMES

While there is no way to prepare any applicant for every question that will be asked of them during an interview, there are certain common interview questions that have a theme to their purpose. What you need to learn is what the employer is really looking to understand about you from the response you provide to their questions. Each question asked of you has a purpose for the employer assuming that they remain compliant and align their interview questions to the essential functions of the position. Interview questions in the traditional or behavioral style may have the same purpose and intent however they will solicit different responses and earlier you learned how to identify the differences and ensure you are using behavioral responses. In this chapter you will get a clearer picture of what a behavioral response is and how to formulate and articulate your answers in this manner. Positions certainly have different essential functions, however most organizations still leverage an interview to gather key competence in a variety of soft skills that will inherently reflect your technical capabilities as well.

Interviewers have a myriad of skills in executing an interview well. There will be interviews in which the questions asked are not relevant, the organization or sequencing of the questions will seem odd and illogical, and the delivery or the questions may be weak causing a tremendous amount of follow up questions due to the interviewer not asking the question in the most effective manner. Regardless of the skills of the interviewer, being prepared and using these techniques and strategies will allow you to articulate who you are and what your experience and competencies are effectively and efficiently. Also, don't be surprised when you are more prepared for the interview than the interviewer.

Before exploring the common themes for interview questions it is important to understand a common error made by an applicant during an interview that is the result of cultural training from their current or previous organizations. Think about your current role, and how you might present a recent project or task to a supervisor or coworker. In your explanation, you might find yourself repeatedly using the word "we" or phrase "our team" as is expected and appropriate. Taking all of the credit for something that you were only a part of is often viewed as inappropriate in an organization. This is because most positions have dependencies or precursors to the tasks and work they perform in the business. The company culture may also focus on collaboration, team work, diversity of thought, and other techniques to bring ideas, people, and tasks together cohesively. In the workforce it is perfect to describe your actions and activities in a group setting using "we" or "our team".

In an interview this is not the case. While there is no "I" in team, there is "I" in interview. Remember that, and train yourself as you practice, plan and prepare for each interview. Certainly there will be times during an interview when you are explaining work you did with or on a team, and that is fine to do. What you need to remember during the presentation of your response is to specifically and in detail call out what you did.

Example

When working at ABC company we designed a new process to produce more widgets in an efficient manner saving the organization time, resources, and most importantly budget. The analysis included a multi-step process in which our team worked with the operations department to identify redundancy and wasted steps. My role on this team and during this project was to gather specific data on the equipment efficiencies, report on the statistical results, summarize findings, and present recommendations to the project leader. In this particular project my recommendations were accepted and the implemented achieving the goals of the initiative.

As you can see above the response certainly gave credit to all of the efforts by other members of the organization. The applicant also effectively articulated their role which also allowed the communication of other skills and expertise such as statistical analysis, report writing, communication, and equipment assessment. The interviewer will receive a solid response and understand what role the applicant had in the work described.

Avoid at all costs using buzzwords you hear about or read on the internet. Since the goal of your responses is to provide depth of expertise in the topic of the question, using surface level buzz words with little to no meaning will not aid you in accomplishing your goal of moving forward in the process and receiving a job offer. One of the most common themes of interview questions concern your strengths and weaknesses. People often cringe at having to answer these questions because they struggle to think of a few words that describe themselves, or they fear exposing weaknesses to a potential employer. I am going to break these two topics down for you and explain what the employer is looking for so that when you are answering you shy away from buzz words and focus on phrases and responses that actually highlight and articulate your experience and competence in areas directly related to the essential functions of the position for which you are interviewing.

The employer understands the KSAOs and competencies necessary for an incumbent to be successful in performing the duties of the role. When they ask an applicant about their strengths, they are not looking for buzz terms like: "team player", "good communicator", "hard worker", "attention to detail", and so on. These responses may be accurate, but if I challenged you to explain what you mean by each of these phrases, you would explain a great deal more than the few words. The guidance and strategy you are getting from this book is going to push you to break free from prior practices and behaviors during an interview and force you into an uncomfortable state so that you can understand a different paradigm of the interview process. If you allow your perspective to change and execute this guidance, you will be in a position to prepare more effectively in order to deliver who you are and what your experience is in an articulate manner.

Staying with strengths and avoidance of buzz words, the all-time worst buzz phrase that leaves me wondering if an applicant can explain any business or technical strength, is "quick learner". Similar to the other phrases noted above, this may be correct, but it is not what you really want or need to communicate to an interviewer. Why are these phrases poor responses during an interview? Because so many applicants use them and the reality is these responses have little to no meaning or value. Think about this concept differently by examining the following question and response. Question - "How much does that car cost?" Answer – "A lot".

The answer may be correct, depending on context for the purchaser, but without the context and without a real dollar amount, the answer contained no value. This is the same for these buzz phrases listed and a myriad of others you can find in guides and websites professing to help people succeed on an interview. Having been on the other side of the table for over two decades, and training hundreds of managers how to analyze and interpret applicant responses, I will tell you these buzz phrases do nothing to increase your chances of getting the job.

Here is why. Take the frequently used "quick learner" phrase. It could mean a plethora of things to whomever the interviewer is and an applicant should take every opportunity to control the interview and leave as little as possible to interpretation. Quick learner may mean the applicant doesn't have the skills or experience but is noting that if given a chance they might be able to learn the job. Another interpretation is they have no strengths to speak of and learned a buzz word to respond to the questions. Yet another interpretation is the applicant can learn the job if there are resources available to train them. In each case the interpretation is not what the applicant intended at all. In fact, there is a deeper more thorough meaning when you claim you are a quick learner. The push back I will provide you here is to not use buzz phrases and instead just tell the interviewer exactly what you mean by the buzz phrase. For example, a very good response to a strength when you would like to knee jerk with quick learner would instead be "When I take on a new role in an existing or new organization I am able to absorb the training and information provided to me rapidly, and assimilate the knowledge with my experience and competencies, so that I am able to execute the tasks I am responsible for at an accelerated pace so as to make a significant impact for the business." Dramatic difference, and it only takes a few additional seconds to respond in this more articulate manner. Does this response imply that you are a quick learner, of course, but it also demonstrates your ability to communicate effectively, that you will be comprehensive with your responses, and that you tie your actions and behaviors back to the success of the business. The interviewer will be very impressed with a more accurate and thorough response compared to the buzz phrases they are so used to hearing from applicants.

Another example we can explore is for the buzz phrase team player. If you are assigned a role that is part of a team, guess what? You are a team player. If you think about any sports team, all of the individuals on the team are team players, but that does not convey the concept or idea you really are attempting to present to an interviewer. What you are most likely attempting to communicate is "In a variety of positions I've held I was either directly part of a team or assigned to work in teams to accomplish projects and initiatives for the company. When working in a team I excel at listening, collaborating, managing conflict, being inclusive, communicating ideas, and providing my support to achieve success for the team and the business." So in other words, a team player but in a practical and realistic and detailed manner. Which response would you like to hear if you were responsible for hiring a new staff member and needed to learn about the individual's strengths?

These examples should begin to provide you clarity on the goal of the interview from the employer and the goal of the applicant in truly providing a clear, concise, and articulate response that represents who you are and what experience and competencies you have to offer the employer.

Some individuals have told me over the years that during an interview they were asked to use three words to describe their strengths, hence they would be unable to use a more articulate response. I disagree, as I would still advise you to respond to the interviewer and state "if you are truly interested in what my strengths are, limiting my response to three words certainly would not benefit your organization in gaining insight into the experience and competencies I have to offer you in this position. I prefer to provide you my three strengths in a brief and concise manner, but limiting to three words does not do me justice nor will it inform you much about who I am. May I proceed?" Now you have just shocked the interviewer, in a positive way, and will be permitted to respond appropriately. This is the same strategy to the interviewer who tells you to describe yourself in five words. It is unrealistic and more importantly the organization who executes interviews in this manner is doing their company a disservice by failing to gather adequate information from an applicant to make an informed decision.

Weaknesses are a different animal with regards to the purpose of asking the question. You handle the response the same, and please stay away from the buzz phrases such as "too much attention to detail", "work too many hours", "I am a perfectionist", or any other phrase the internet and others will tell you are actually positive attributes or behaviors but can be viewed as negative to answer the question. What a waste of time and effort on your part as an applicant to use a buzz phrase when this question, about weaknesses, is more powerful than the strengths. How do we learn, by making mistakes. We all make mistakes, and we all learn something from them.

I am going to let you in on a little secret. The question is not to expose the applicant to being human and making mistakes, or being weak in an area so they can reject you. The question, if used strategically by the employer, seeks to understand the honesty of the applicant, the humility of the applicant, and how the applicant handles weaknesses as a professional. What does this mean for you? Think about riding a bike, and how many times when learning you fell off the bike before your body mastered the balance necessary to ride and eventually after getting back on that bike repeatedly you mastered the skill. Therefore, you faced a weakness in your life, the inability to ride a bike, but you trained and practices, received guidance and direction, and eventually succeeded, correct?

When an employer is asking you about your weaknesses, you can respond in two ways. First, you can explain a few skills or competencies in which you are not fully experienced with related to the role demonstrating humility and honesty. This is respectable, but may not achieve success and more importantly doesn't demonstrate a critical piece of what the employer is looking to hear from you. The second method to responding would be to identify a real weakness you "had" in the recent past that you have overcome. This is the real key to the question, and the ability to articulate this well certainly positions you for success in this part of the interview. For example, assume you were unsuccessful in the past at facilitating a staff meeting, but after research, training, coaching, and practice you were able to overcome the task by mastering the skills you were lacking to achieve success. The response might sound something like this "In recent years as I advanced in a prior organization, I was responsible for facilitating weekly staff meetings with a team of four direct reports. Having never done this before I was nervous and ineffective during the first few meetings. I researched strategies for executing team facilitation, identified and completed a training class on the topic, and sought the advice of professional mentors for the coaching I needed. After practicing the techniques and strategies learned I gained mastery over this competency and confidence in my effectiveness in facilitating staff meetings. I approach all of my weaknesses in this manner, by first identifying the gap and taking action to resolve it to achieve my goals."

What a difference a little planning, thought, and articulation will do to a response. Think about this, you have answered the question presented to you by sharing a weakness, but you also demonstrated what you do when you identify a weakness to overcome it and achieve success. Therefore, you demonstrated actions and behaviors that are indicative of how you will take on similar obstacles and challenges in the future. This is a fantastic demonstration of using a traditional question to provide a behavioral answer in an effective manner. This skill takes time and practice to master, but I assure you when you begin to think about all of your answers in this new paradigm your interviewing will be improved and your chances for success increased.

Experienced interviewers will not always make it easy for you as an applicant to know the goal of their questions, especially when it comes to potentially negative topics such as weaknesses or failures. I mastered asking the weakness question by spinning the question into developmental topics. For example, instead of asking what the applicant's weakness was, I would ask "tell me about one or two skills or competencies you are looking to gain or develop if you were to join our organization?" Sure this question sounds less intimidating, however it leads an applicant to speak about where they are lacking a skill or expertise and competence that may relate to the role for which they applied. The purpose of asking the question this way is to place the applicant at ease and speak about development versus weaknesses, which is a more comfortable topic for the applicant. The reality, as you may have already perceived, is the question is exactly the same and the employer is seeking to understand what weaknesses the applicant has. If yo are on the receiving end of this question from a development perspective you want to articulate your answer in similar fashion to the question of weaknesses. Share a skill or competence you identified or became aware of in the past in which you needed development and share what you did about it and how you overcame the challenge in your career. This way you demonstrate self-awareness, humility, and the ability to resolve skill short falls by pursuing and executing professional development.

A major mistake often made by applicants is replying to the weakness or development question with the answer "I don't have any weaknesses" or "There is nothing I need to develop." A response such as this is ill advised, as it reflects an attitude and mindset that implies you do not reflect on your own career, skills and competence honestly and with purpose. You also present to the interviewer as if you do not ever make mistakes, and you know everything leaving no room for growth. This should never be the case as you want to demonstrate humility and the characteristic of being a lifelong learner, always willing and open to professional growth and development to increase your ability to contribute to an organization and achieve success.

The next theme of questions has to do with success and failures in your career. The concept of this theme is parallel to the strength and weakness questions. Most people can easily share the success stories of their career. The greatest accomplishments, the best sales year, the most impactful contribution, and so on. If you had to stop reading right now and come up with a success story from your current or most recent position, you could do it relatively easily. Therefore, my guidance and strategy for a success story is to plan and prepare several stories ahead of time that are relevant and supportive of your candidacy for the position you applied for. Do not share a story that fails to highlight skills and competencies the employer is looking for in the role you applied for, specifically, relate to the essential functions of the role and the job requirements for the position. Use your time telling the story to cover as many job requirements as possible to demonstrate past experience and competence performing the tasks. This approach is much more effective than attempting to tell an interviewer you can do the work. Demonstrating you have done the work before is highly effective.

Questions about prior failed efforts, tasks, projects, or initiatives may be extremely daunting during an interview. Applicants are easily intimidated by these because again similar to a weakness, they are being asked to reveal an error, mistake, gap in skill or competence, and to be humble and honest. Answering this question incorrectly can lead to a disaster of an interview. You need not worry about these questions as you are going to be able to reveal more information and demonstrate behaviors the employer is seeking with a question about a past failure than a question about your successes if you prepare and execute your response appropriately.

Remember that the employer is looking to gain information about you from each questions, and the employer is looking to see both what your answer is and analyze how you answered the question. Another little secret to share with you is the employer is attempting to determine during the interview how you are going to handle problems, challenges, obstacles, and failures as an employer of their organization. Therefore it is critical you answer this question effectively by demonstrating past behaviors. The employer knows that you are bound to make a mistake, encounter an obstacle, or experience a failure in their workforce and it is their responsibility to attempt to hire individuals who not only have the requisite experience and competencies, but also the demonstrated behavior to deal with failure situations. Recall our earlier presentation of the behavioral interviewing style, in which past work performance of an individual is indicative of future work performance. If you can effectively demonstrate on an interview your experience overcoming a failure or challenge in the past it will instill confidence in the employer you will handle similar situations appropriately and effectively in their organization.

The key to this strategy is to highlight at the end of the response what you learned from the experience and what you would do differently in the future. When you master articulating both the failure story and the learning from the experience during the interview this type of question will no longer be intimidating and instead become a refreshing opportunity to highlight your professional growth and development while sharing technical, business, and soft skills you have applicable to the position you applied for. As an example, below is a response to a question about past failures.

Example

Certainly, in my most recent organization I was part of a project team in which we had an established budget and timeline to redesign a procedure to meet customer needs. Unfortunately, there were several factors that led to the failure, ranging from resources, budget, timeline, and stakeholder expectations. Leadership reduced the length of time to complete the procedure due to external factors beyond our team's control forcing us to modify the procedure if we wanted to remain on budget. The change appeared to work for our department, however upon final recommendation we realized that the distribution center would be unable to package the product with the recommended changes to the procedure efficiently causing delays. Ultimately, the project failed and we had to start over with more consideration for the internal distribution stake-

holder who would be impacted by our efforts. My major learning from this project was the need for increased communication and collaboration with all stakeholders during the project. Once we were more inclusive with the other department the second attempt was more successful than we had expected the first procedure to be and I have been applying better communication and collaboration techniques with stakeholders on all subsequent projects.

This response example has all of the components of an honest response, detailed and comprehensive, inclusive of the failure and the learning. Finally, the response follows a critical point made early on regarding SAR. This response explained the situation faced by the employee, the actions taken, and the end results. Perfect technique for a behavioral response. We are going to briefly explore SAR more before we go on to the next theme.

Early in chapter 8 you learned about a resume technique to represent your experience with SAR. SAR is situation, action, and results. Once you begin answering the more complex questions through behavioral demonstration you must articulate your responses using SAR. During an interview you must focus on the answering the question based on your past work and academic experience as well as general knowledge and competence gained during your life. When you plan and prepare for the interview you should be writing down several success stories and several failure stories so they come to mind easily during the interview. Once you complete the step of identifying the stories you would want to share that are applicable to the job you applied for, the next part of the planning process is organizing into SAR.

Think about your response in this manner, past state, action, current state. In other words, what was the situation in the past and what were you tasked with accomplishing in your role. Then you describe what action you personally took while detailing the skills, technologies, systems, and competencies you used to execute those actions. Finally, you describe the results and not just by stating it worked or that the effort was a success. You want to explain the impact on the organization or business by the successful completion of the initiative, effort, project, or task. Similar to how you must explain the learning in a failure story, you explain the business impact in a success story. Doing so effectively represents a higher level of business acumen and it is impressive for a potential employer to hear an applicant reflect how their work directly impacts the business. It shows the employer you understand the business landscape, how your efforts contribute to the business model and delivery of products or services to the customers.

The next theme we are going to review is process improvement. Many years ago you would find suggestion boxes in most companies for employees to present recommendations to management and leadership. With the evolution and development of improved technology and organizational engagement the old basic concept of a suggestion became the basis for continuous process improvement initiatives. Believe it or not there is no difference in making a suggestion or proposing a process improvement.

An employer seeks to hire individuals who not only want to join the organization and work, but who also wants to share new ideas on how to accomplish tasks and goals of the business. Employers hire new perspectives, innovation and creativity in addition to the core skills and experience necessary to perform a job. Keep this in mind when you are interviewing, so that when the question is presented in which you recognize they want you to provide an example of when you were part of a process improvement you will know what they are asking you.

Strategy for answering a process improvement question is slightly more complex than just telling the interviewer you had an idea, presented it, the company did it, and it was a big success. That would not be the most effective manner to respond. A suggestion or process improvement has several steps and you will want to detail each step so the interviewer not only hears what a wonderful recommendation you made, but they are presented with demonstrated experience carrying out the process appropriately. The steps generally include: (1) Identification of a problem or a gap that needs to be fixed or improved; (2) Development of a business case proposal which should be evidence based in which you outlined the current state of the situation and various options to take action to resolve the problem; (3) Presentation of the business case to supervisor or management, including titles and size of audience; (4) Persuasion or influence communication skills to obtain support for the recommendation; (5) Development and Implementation of the recommendation; and (6) Results of the process improvement or change.

When explaining a process improvement initiative the end result does not need to be success. In fact, since not every suggestion can be implemented in a business, most fail in achieving approval. This means the question is really about your understanding of the process, and demonstration of experience carrying it out in prior roles. Be certain to detail how you identified the problem and what skills, experience, and competence allowed you to do so. The business case is generally a presentation, report, or analysis that you provide to a member of management who has the authority to approve taking the recommended actions for the business. The recommendation should never be based on the fact that "you know it will work better" but rather data and evidence of studying and researching the problem to determine the best possible solutions. Be sure to include what other functions or departments you worked with to demonstrate collaboration and inclusion during the process. Explain who you made presentations to at what level to demonstrate working with peers and management at various levels of authority. If at first your proposal was rejected, this will allow you to explain how your communication skills were executed to influence or persuade your audience to see your perspective and approve moving forward with your ideas. If you were involved in the actual development or implementation of the solution you can include that, but this part may not have happened yet, or you might now be involved in these stage of the project. Finally, what was the outcome if the recommendations were implemented? If it was successful, be sure to detail how and what success meant for the business. It is okay if the project failed to deliver what it promised, just treat the response as a failure story and note what you learned from the experience.

All organizations are made up of people, resulting in communication exchanges and discussions between individuals who may not necessarily agree all the time. Our next theme is conflict management, which is not the same as conflict resolution. Conflict resolution is a process by which the conflict is stopped, whereas conflict management is a process by which conflict is leveraged and utilized as a business activity to enhance communication and diversity of thought.

The purpose of an employer asking an applicant about conflict management is twofold. First, to examine past communication behaviors and second, to understand how the applicant will work through conflict challenges in their organization. Since conflict is expected to happen it is a critical skill and competence to demonstrate success management when the situation arises.

So what do I mean by conflict? I do not mean a personal disagreement between two coworkers, or a verbal argument that has nothing to do with the business itself. These situations are not something you should be sharing during an interview ever. Many applicants jump directly to a personal issue with another employee, which is more about an employee relations situation than a business situation in which conflict existed. Consider conflict as something appropriate and useful in the workplace. For example, if you and your supervisor are discussing a project or task, and the supervisor states "we should go left" and you say "I think we should go right" you have just created and will experience conflict. How you manage this situation is exactly what an interviewer is seeking to understand, as your past work behavior will be indicative of handling conflict in their organization.

You will want to prepare a few different situations and example that you can share with the interviewer that highlight your skills. Regardless of the example you provide, be certain to include the following pieces of information in your response: (1) Describe the business situation and specify what was in conflict; (2) describe what actions you took during the interaction, including steps you took to listen and understand the perspective of the other individual; (3) explain how you analyzed the other perspectives; (4) describe how you were reflective on your own point of view; (5) describe what steps you took to achieve a win-win-win situation for you, the other individual involved, and the business; and (6) the ultimate end result of the conflict event. What is most important about the situation you describe is the manner in which you articulate your ability to be open to other perspectives and ideas. That you do not simply force others to only listen to you, and that you are not always right. In fact, some of the best responses I have heard to this question include the applicant realizing their own perspective was incomplete or not the most effective and the result of the exchange was learning and growth. However you chose to respond to a question about conflict management do not articulate yourself as being perfect or having all the answers, that will never make the same impression with the employer as an individual who can demonstrate their ability to be humble and willing to hear the ideas of others.

Employees with strong business ethics are valued across industries. Determining an individual's moral and ethical work behaviors is not always easy, but employers will do their best during an interview to ascertain whatever information possible to aid in the decision making process. When talking about business ethics, organizations hope to hire an applicant with values similar to those of the desired culture, and leadership of the organization. This is not easy to accomplish through a single or even multiple interviews. Strategies and techniques are implemented both in the traditional and behavioral style to solicit examples of work behavior that could be indicative of the business ethics of the applicant.

When asked to provide an example of an ethical dilemma or situation faced in your career, the worst possible answer is "I've never had an ethical dilemma in the workforce." Why? Because that answer would not be accurate if you truly analyzed the question and understood what the employer is trying to understand about you. A company wants to do their best to ensure every employee complies with policies, procedures, rules, processes, and standards established by the organization. This inquiry seeks to go even further than just compliance on the surface, it moves to the core issue of action and behaviors by an employee once they are privy to, observe, or become aware of wrong doing in the workplace.

If you struggle with the term "ethical dilemma" you are not alone. Immediately many applicants become defensive and concerned they are being asked to tell the employer when and what they have done wrong in the past. Some believe they are being asked to reveal something wrong with the employees of the current or past employer. Neither of these lines of thought are accurate. The employer is seeking to understand you, the applicant, and how you act and behave in the face of an ethical dilemma in the context of business ethics. Will you do the right thing for the company? That is the core question they want to uncover when asking about business ethics.

There are two examples I have provided to applicants for years that are simple to understand and help you grasp the concept.

Example One – Ethical Dilemma

You are checking out at a local retail store and you pay the cashier for the $8.50 of products with a $10.00 bill. The cashier, thinking you gave them a $20.00 bill provides you with

$11.50 in change. You now have an ethical dilemma, in which you have to decide what to do using good judgment and moral values. You can advise the teller and return the extra $10.00 or you can leave the store. This situation boils down to an internal decision made by the customer and no one may know what happened.

Example Two – Ethical Dilemma
You pack up your belongings to leave work for the day, and as you walk past the supply room you observe one of your peers taking various business supplies and placing them into their personnel backpack. Eye contact is made with the employee. You wait a few minutes down the hallway and see the employee as they prepare to walk right out of the office with the stolen supplies. You have a decision to make as this ethical dilemma unfolds. You know this employee, have for years, and recognize that any action you take may not only result in action by the employer against the employee, but also the relationship may become strained or cease. A major decision is in front of you and your ethics and morals are being tested.

In both examples the individual must make a decision that could lead to embarrassment and possible negative consequences. What an interviewer is seeking during the interview is demonstrated appropriate behavior when these situations are faced. The reality is every employee at one point or another is exposed to or faces an ethical dilemma in the workplace, ranging from small minor policy violations or infraction to major issues like fraud or harassment. What is important for you as the applicant to understand is what the goal of the question is. The goal is to determine how you, the applicant, handled these types of situations in the past which may be indicative of how you will behave and act in the future at their company when an ethical situation confronts you. We don't ask for these situations to happen, they just do, and how we respond is critical.

When responding, you want to be clear on what the ethical situation was so the audience understands how it was a problem in your organization. Then you need to address what actions you took, who you communicated with, and what the end result was that you are aware of. Presenting a story in which you observed an ethical situation that could damage the business and ignored it, or failed to report it or take action will hurt your chances of success. Therefore be considerate of your response and focus on situations in which you took timely and appropriate action, confronted and or notified members of management, and supported the resolution to protect the company. Your past behavior in handling an ethical dilemma will be a fundamental indicator to the interviewer of how you might handle a similar situation in their company.

The next theme is technical skills as they relate to software applications and tools used to perform your role. This is not the technical skills you possess in your profession. For example, your competence and mastery of the Microsoft Office Suite of applications, Enterprise Resource Planning systems, Human Resources Information Systems, Customer Relationship Management Systems, Sales Automation, Financial Tools and Systems, etc. Your resume should list all of these technical skills and they should be embedded throughout the document. During the interview you will often be asked to speak about your competence in using these technologies, especially if the essential functions of the role require it. This is where caution is suggested and coaching is needed. Some applicants will make blanket broad statements about their level of mastery that can get them in trouble, and most often it is unintentional. For example, when asked the experience level with Microsoft Excel, some reply "I am an expert, on a scale of 1-10 I give myself a 10. I teach others how to use it, I am the go to person." This is a nice answer, but could easily have holes blown through it if you are not careful. Place the response in context for a minute, and think about what the person might have used the application for. Perhaps budgeting, forecasting, forms, analysis, statistics, something else. The response lacks humility and opens the door for someone with more expertise to erode the response which hurts you during the interview. What an applicant needs to recognize is that while they are great at using the technology for their current purposes, another organization may use the same technology differently or in a more complex manner. Their mastery may be limited and failing to understand this fact can hurt an applicant.

I try to remind people that in the position they held, performing the duties and tasks assigned, they might have gained extensive mastery over using the technology for a specific purpose. However, the suite of Microsoft applications can handle entire business operations and functions, and there is almost always more to learn and master for other tasks and duties an employee may need to perform. Therefore, when responding you should either be humble with the response or at a minimum add context to the response. For example "I believe my skills in MS Excel are a 10 in using basic formulae, data entry, and analysis of financial reporting. However my skills beyond these functions are limited only due to the lack of necessity in performing additional tasks with the technology."

When providing information about the various systems you have experience with, rather than just stating the type of system, or the name which may or may not be recognizable depending on home grown internal systems that exist, be sure to explain what you use the system for and how. Include information such as for entering information, retrieving or reporting information, analysis, transaction processing, or communication. Adding information in your response related to the frequency of use and if you review and approve the work in the system of other employees is beneficial. If you provide training to others on the processes, if you were involved in drafting procedures related to the system, or if you were involved in the selection, design, and implementation of the system be sure in all cases to detail what your role was for the interviewer.

We are going to wrap up this chapter by addressing a favorite question theme of mine and that is about the applicant's goals. The question can be formulated various ways, such as "what do you want to do in the future?" or "What are your future plans?" or even something simple like "Do you have any professional goals?" As I have done throughout this text, let us explore the purpose of this question by an employer.

Let your mind wander for a second and imagine yourself as the owner of a business and you are hiring an employee to help you achieve your business goals. Fundamentally, there is already a reason and purpose for this position in the company, and the essential functions as well as the desired impact and contributions are planned and anticipated. Your task so to speak as the interviewer is to now match the knowledge, skills, experience, and other characteristics of the applicants with both the minimum qualifications of the position and the expected work performance and behaviors of an incumbent in the role. Taking this concept further, when an employer hires an employee, there may also be the long term desire to hire someone capable of growing with the organization to take on greater responsibility and contribute at an increasing rate year after year. These goals of the employer translate well into a simple and very traditional interview style question about the future.

Often I have asked the question "What is your 2-5 year goal?" Keep in mind from the information above, that the employer is seeking to understand from the applicants perspective where the match is not just today but over the course of time.

Would you be surprised to know that more than 75% of the time the response fails to answer the question satisfactorily if at all? Here are some responses I have received over the past few decades.

- Retire.
- Go back to school.
- Be president of your company.
- Take a vacation.
- Make more money.
- To have stability.
- Learn something new.
- Send my children to college.
- Do something fun.

The critical failure in these responses are they are unrelated to the reason you are interviewing with this employer. In other words, what does any of this have to do with the position you applied for, and how does this response impact your ability to demonstrate you are the best applicant for the job? The employer is exposed to these answers quite frequently and therefore it is very simple to leave a positive lasting impression with an appropriate response.

Focus your thinking on the process itself. The interview, the offer, the position, the promotion or advancement opportunities, the ultimate position or role you want with the organization, and so on. Keep the response focused not only on what you want, but the value your goals deliver to the employer. Whatever your response becomes, no matter how strong the urge is to use something similar to the ineffective list above, start with the primary goal of "obtaining a job offer for the position you are interviewing for" and then demonstrate to the interviewer a logical and rational approach to goal setting, expectations, and motivation.

Perhaps you are interviewing for a supervisor position, and the hierarchy of the company includes managers, directors, vice presidents, and so on across various departments and functional areas. The following response is to a goals oriented question that will demonstrate everything you want the employer to hear and understand about your strategic planning and goal setting capabilities.

My primary goal at this time is to demonstrate the necessary expertise, competence, and workplace behaviors to secure an offer from your company. Beyond that, as this is a supervisory role I will dedicate my efforts to achieve the goal of career advancement within the organization seeking to achieve the role of manager in two years. Prior to moving vertically in the organization, as a manager I will set a goal to master various functional aspects of the different business units to increase my contributions outside my current department, and then utilize this breadth of knowledge to take on greater responsibility as a director when the timing is mutually beneficial to the company.

There is a very distinct difference not only in the substance of the response, but the method and manner in which the applicant can articulate this to the employer speaks volumes about other skills as well. Under no circumstances should you ever tell an employee you have no goals. Under no circumstances should your response fail to include the position for which you are interviewing for as a short term immediate goal. Neglecting to apply this guidance creates an immediate mismatch in the mind of the interviewer bringing into question why you even applied for the job.

If you go back and think about your short introduction and summary, there will be times where you are selling the employer on why you are a great applicant and why you want to work at their business. To not take the time and plan ahead for the goal question ensuring that you have an elegant and articulate response to tie the interest together with the goal is a mistake that could cost you advancement in the interview and recruitment process.

CHAPTER ELEVEN

STRATEGY – DURING THE INTERVIEW

You have arrived prepared to answer questions, present yourself in the best light, and accomplish your goal of getting the job offer. Now it is time to execute your plan and strategy and interact with members of the company assigned to eliminate or advance you in the process. All the preparation in the world may not ensure a smooth interview because the employer is the random link in the process. What I mean by this is you might find during your career that you are more prepared and trained on the interview process than the individual sitting across from you. This is just a fact that you must digest and recognize so that you may take control of the interview at appropriate times to share your information and demonstrate your fit for the role. Regardless of the interviewer's preparation, this chapter will provide you with key techniques, strategies, and tips to keep your head in the game, stay focused, and perform at your best.

If you are being interviewed by only one person face to face, even if it is a series of interviews during the process, be certain to make appropriate eye contact while listening to questions presented, and during the delivery of your response. The more effective you are at captivating the interest of the interviewer the better you will be able to read the expressions and mannerisms of the interviewer and determine if more or less is needed from current of future responses. This does not mean stare at the person, this guidance is to ensure you are not looking at the floor, ceiling, or everywhere else in the room reflecting a lack of confidence and preparation for engaging in direct communication and dialogue with the employer.

As repeated throughout this book, in as many responses as possible apply SAR to give context, breadth, and depth to your response. Often applicants believe they are not permitted to write anything down or take notes during an interview. This is not correct, and unless specifically advised that you may not do so, bring paper and a writing instrument to take notes during the interview. These notes should not only be questions asked or information they give you about the position. Your notes should include topics you want to cover, systems or technologies they mention that you can incorporate into your responses, details about the interviewer you want to connect with, and reminders for yourself on the delivery of responses.

I strongly encourage having notes already prepared to aid you in keeping focused and highlighting key experience and knowledge you want to present during the interview. Use the third or fourth page of a notepad to conceal these notes from the top page where you take notes during the interview. By conceal, I mean do not have a sloppy array of chicken scratch exposed to the interviewer(s) which would look unprofessional. Organize neatly your notes and have them accessible for use during the interview.

Do not read directly from the notes without making eye contact and demonstrating that you are simply referring to a term or phrase that will aid you in responding or asking a question. Having a notepad is a wonderful tool to calm yourself down, present yourself reminders, and to increase your ability to handle multi part questions. Whenever a question is presented with multiple parts you certainly want to address each part of the question. Human nature may be to begin answering the last part of the question and tangents and other distractions, such as interviewer follow up, may take up time and migrate you away mentally from responding fully to the intended question. Therefore, make a quick note about the parts of the question asked and then refer back to this note as you near the end of your response so you can extend your answer and continue meeting the employer's expectations with regards to the question.

This approach of taking notes is also a technique to allow you to calm down and think about a response before you knee jerk and regret the answer. As you have already learned, some questions have deeper real purpose than the surface question presented. If you do not take time to understand the question you will not answer it properly. Writing down the question or key words and concepts about the question will allow you time to digest the information. Most interviewers will not rush you to answer a question and value thoughtfulness in a response. This technique is also good when you do not know the answer, so you can remind yourself to be honest and explain you do not have an answer while also providing transferrable experience that may keep you in the process.

Not every question will need to be written down and instead a strategy should be implemented to take note to demonstrate an increased level of interest and enthusiasm in the information you are receiving. When an applicant takes no notes and seem to verbalize enthusiasm but there is limited observable action to align with what is presented verbally a disconnect can happen. Take every opportunity and apply every strategy to maximize the limited time and exposure you have to present to the employer who you are and what you can do for them.

In several chapters we addressed transferrable skills and the need to be able to recognize the true question presented and be inclusive in your response of a variety of competencies you have. Again, during the interview proactively develop the context of your situation and leverage the action and response aspects of the reply to incorporate other knowledge, skills, abilities, and characteristics that add value to the employer and demonstrate depth of expertise.

A serious flaw in some applicant responses is a total failure to answer the question asked. This happens all too often, and is generally the result of trying to have "canned" responses for an interview. Prepare and master who you are from a competence and experience perspective so that you can digest and interpret the question presented and then answer accordingly. While some interviewers will certainly go on a tangent as they learn more about you, it can be detrimental to the applicant to interact in similar fashion. Each tangent you initiate and pursue damages your credibility as an applicant and further diminishes the time available to present well to the employer. I have directly observed an applicant moving down the path of a tangent and corner themselves into presenting non-relevant information that actually damaged their presentation of their skills and experience.

For example, many applicants begin speaking about other team members or co-workers and then reveal their perspectives of the people versus staying on target about the work experience and how they performed the work. This can open the door to follow up questions unrelated to the essential functions of the role or corner you into struggling to explain yourself. This is not where you want to be during an interview and certainly isn't a strategy to retain as much control of the exchange as possible. The message here is to avoid tangents.

In preparing for an interview we spoke about having the right attire and planning your wardrobe. Now that you are in the interview, what you want to think about is your posture and mannerisms to create a presence of professionalism. This is accomplished by observing the interviewer and gaining a perspective of how they are sitting, how they are gesturing, and whether or not they are leaning on the desk or table. You want to sit up tall and confident with good posture in your back and shoulders. You should find a comfortable position for your hands so that you have them folded in your lap or on the table in front of you. This accomplishes a few things, most importantly it helps you avoid being fidgety and removes the opportunity to show off any nervousness. Another advantage of hand placement in this manner is to remind yourself about gesturing. If you normally speak a great deal with your hands this is a technique to force you to speak to the audience versus using your hands excessively. It is appropriate to communicate with both verbal and body language, but do not let the body language overtake the interview or mislead the employer due to body language not matching verbal responses.

If the interviewer presents comfortably and crosses their legs or leans back, do not be afraid to do the same during the interview in an effort to remain comfortable. It is appropriate and acceptable to request a glass of water if you did not bring your own bottle or container beverage to drink during the interview. The goal is to remain focused and relaxed so you can present your best throughout the interview.

When you receive a question that either has stumped you or you do not feel prepared immediately to answer, a very good technique to apply is asking the interviewer to repeat the question. Once it is repeated, parrot back key portions of the question and then take a moment to either write it down or breathe before you begin responding. This allows you to process the question thoroughly and formulate a response without feeling rushed. This technique should also reduce stress or nervousness with questions you do not feel prepared for.

Upon arrival at the interview, and at the conclusion of the exchange with the interviewer, be sure to thank the individual for taking time out of their day to meet with you and share information about the position and the organization.

As final strategic guidance for you during an interview I present to you a question. When does the interview start and when does it end? If your answer is when you sit down with the interviewer and when you leave the interviewer, you are wrong! It is a common mistake to view the interview in the finite space of time when you are in front of the employer's interviewer or interview panel. This approach can certainly leave you without a job offer and wondering what went wrong, but you will never find out. Certainly the interview documentation based on questions asked and answered are what makes it to the recruitment folder for record keeping purposes. However from the moment you arrived at the employer site to the moment you leave the site you are being observed and monitored and all gathered information is presented in some manner to the hiring authority so they can arrive at an appropriate decision for their company and the position.

Upon arrival, if there is security, they should be viewed as a potential input into the process. How you treat and interact with them, how you speak and carry yourself, and how you respect the work they perform for the company. Next you have the reception area, where another employee will welcome you and interact with you most generally with directions and update on the process. If you don't believe they have input you are very mistaken, and not just before the interview. If the same or other individuals are present during your exit, they observe how you react and handle the interview and often capture everything you say to them. This becomes fodder and information often used by hiring authorities to determine the culture fit and communication behaviors and abilities of the applicant. You do not want to present wonderfully during the question and answer exchange and fail miserably during other interactions that take place during the full interview.

This advice is not condoning or advocating that these practices by employers are necessarily inside the legal context of fair and compliant hiring practices since the observed interaction and behaviors may have nothing to do with the essential functions of the position. Nonetheless, this book is about practical advice and reality. Do not think for one minute that these activities and interactions go unnoticed, and therefore until you are off the company site conduct yourself as if the interview is still going on.

CHAPTER TWELVE

STRATEGY –
CLOSING THE INTERVIEW

The questions have finally ended and you sense the meeting is coming to a close. It is time to implement a number of strategies to take some control of the process and close the interview. There are a number of tasks you want to be sure to accomplish before the employer shuts the meeting down. Having the courage to execute these tasks is not always easy, simply because of the desire to please the employer, meet their expectations, and get a job offer. Applicants put themselves in a position of weakness when the interview wraps up and that is not where you want to be, regardless of the ultimate outcome.

Did you take every and any opportunity offered to you by the interviewer to ask questions about the interviewer, the position, and the company? It is rare for an interview to close without the question "Do you have any questions?" being presented to the applicant. This is where nerves and anxiety get the best of many people and they reply "no" and end the meeting. This is a serious mistake on your part as an applicant, it demonstrates a lack of confidence, a lack of enthusiasm or interest, and a lack of planning. This is the best time to refer to your notes and regroup so you can take control and end the interview on your terms and in a manner you wish related to information you want out of the process. Remember, an interview is two sided. The employer is seeking to learn about you and how you fit the role, and you must be evaluating the employer to determine if the company, culture, and work environment is one you will be successful in.

Sell yourself. Plain and simple, at the end you should have your elevator pitch ready to present a thirty second summary of who you are, why you are the best applicant for the position, how you would add value to the company, and highlight your level of interest. In recent years I included a question in all of my interviews that was intentionally designed to help the applicant achieve this task. Certainly they did not always realize that, and the disappointment from our interview panel(s) was apparent when the applicant did not take advantage of it. I would ask "Is there anything else you would like to share with us about your professional experience that we have not covered here today that is relevant to the position you have applied for?" Think about how generic and open ended this question is. If you are faced with a similar question during an interview, do not skip the opportunity just given to you in presenting who you are and articulating why your experience is a match for the position at their company.

Referring again back to preparation in chapter 4, be sure you have several questions prepared for each interviewer during the process that will elicit different information that will aid you in making a decision about the job for which you applied. This is the time if not already covered to present these questions and obtain information you want to know about the company.

I cannot tell you how many times in my career as a recruiting consultant and staffing firm owner that an applicant would fail to own any of the interview and looked to me to tell them how they performed during the interview. Imagine for a moment an applicant shaking hands with the interview team, walking out to their car, and calling me to ask "How did I do?" It was absolutely ridiculous in my mind and there was little to no logic in the process. Certainly at some point in time the employer would call my firm and communicate if an offer was to be made. But that is irrelevant to how well the applicant actually did in answering the questions, and it is far too late in the process to challenge or correct any deficiencies of the applicant in their responses. This situation was *the* catalyst in my development of an interview preparation for job applicants in the first place.

We might all agree that there is one piece of information each and every job applicant wants to know at the conclusion of an interview. How did they do? Unfortunately, and this becomes scary to many applicants, there is a very simple way to find out during the closing process of the interview. Having read this far in the book I am confident you realize now that the solution is to ask the interviewer. What a frightful proposition, ask the potential employer who perhaps holds your future in their hands how you did during the interview? YES! Before you do, there are definitely reminders here that I will expand upon to help you establish the appropriate expectations related to asking an employer how you did on the interview. You will learn one strategy to ask the question but the important thing is to ask, how you ask is critical but less important because the reality is you will either ask and get feedback or you will not ask. Executing the former will leave you in a state of having more knowledge and insight, doing the latter will force you to scratch your hear, worry, stress, and wonder if you will ever hear back from the employer. Further, if rejected you may never know why.

First, setting expectations around the inquiry is important. The interviewer may or may not be trained and experienced enough to know how to answer your question. Some well-trained interviewers with human resource or management experience will move in stride, not miss a beat, and respond to the inquiry. Others may think it is illegal or inappropriate to share with an applicant how they did during the interview. Regardless, you must establish realistic expectations around asking the question.

The employer has no obligation to tell you how you did during the interview and even very limited obligation to explain their hiring decision unless challenged. So when asking, know this strategy is more about observing reaction, interpreting responses, and satisfying your instinct to know where you stand.

When asking how you did, recognize that you are really only asking how you did in relationship to the questions asked and the responses provided. Do not think you are asking if you got the next interview, the job offer, etc. More than 95% of the time they will never tell you this information at this time because other steps in the process need to take place from a human resource perspective. So your expectations must be focused and practical to seek understanding about how your responses met their expectations for what they asked. You must be aware that they should not, and generally will not compare you to other applicants, and if they have additional interviewing to conduct for the position there is no way for them to know if you are the best applicant yet. So in the end, understand the question is strategic to gain knowledge you would otherwise not have if you fail to ask.

Most people have difficulty lying on the spot and hiding their emotions or facial expressions and mannerisms. Therefore, asking how you did at the end face to face when looking the interviewer in the eye will be revealing. How skilled you become at understanding the response depends on your communication skills and emotional intelligence.

Even if you are told you did wonderful on the interview, take that information for what it is worth and be honest with yourself in this regard. What are you being told *really*? That you handled yourself well and answered all of the questions. That does not mean they will hire you, that you are the best applicant, most qualified, etc. Simply, you can feel good about how you executed the interview process.

Moving on to the actual question you should ask and why, I developed this question many years ago for the clients I represented on interviews and it became very successful in putting control and confidence into the hands of the applicant. It also eliminated the calls where they asked me how they did in a meeting I was not present for. The question is designed to be a yes or no answer, on purpose. The question forces a response, and based on the response you are prepared with the follow up question to move the process forward.

From what we've discussed so far today, is there anything that would prevent me from moving forward in the process?

Starting with the answer of "No" from the interviewer, you then immediately follow up with another question so that you gain insight and influence the next steps towards success.

Great. Then what is the next step in the process and would you like to schedule that now?

This allows you to engage the employer and set up time for the next interview, provide your availability, or gain insight into when you could expect a verbal or written offer. Obviously this is the more favorable response you all want to hear. It is also the easiest answer for the employer to give without having any commitment to the applicant.

If the answer is "Yes", the individual providing the answer may even articulate what went wrong or where you missed their expectations. This is great news for you, because you then have an opportunity to address the gap and present more information in an effort to satisfy the expectation. This is not easy for an applicant, because you have just been told you may not move forward in the process, but the feedback is invaluable now and into the future. Based on what is shared, offer to provide additional information about your experience and performance competencies to address the gap, highlighting that during the interview there may have been a miscommunication or misunderstanding of the goal of a question, and you appreciate the opportunity to address it now. After providing the additional information, ask the same question again, adding that now that you have provide more information, is there anything else that would prevent you from moving forward in the process. If the answer is now "No", you have succeeded in this exchange and have a better feel for where you stand. If the answer is still "Yes", you must use your own judgment and discern if you are comfortable with the reality of a rejection, and accept the feedback and move on. Do not keep pressing when it is apparent there is no fit from the employer's perspective.

At the conclusion of your exchange, wrap up the meeting by asking each member of the interview panel or the individual interviewer for their business card and/or contact information. You may not always receive it, especially if the process was coordinated by a third party, an administrative staff member, or the human resources department. Don't expect to receive the information, but if you do you will be in a better position for activities after the interview which are covered in the next chapter.

CHAPTER THIRTEEN

STRATEGY –
AFTER THE INTERVIEW

You have succeeded in completing the interview with the employer. Perhaps you obtained insight into the next steps, and now you are ready to thank the employer one last time for providing you the opportunity to meet with them and explore their vacant position.

There are certainly a wide range of views on how to handle a thank you correspondence to the employer. First understand that the employer has absolutely no obligation to read, review, distribute, or consider anything you include in the thank you communication. This fact drives the guidance you are about to receive on the topic of thank you letters and communications.

With current advancements in technology and electronic communication systems, you will have an opportunity to send the thank you letter almost immediately to the employer. From a strategic perspective, you do not want to get into your vehicle in the parking lot or hop on the bus or train home and email the thank you. That may be too quick and demonstrate desperation as well as overkill in enthusiasm, especially if the interviews are continuing throughout the day. Instead, when you are home, review your notes from the interview, digest the information provided to you, and relax. Then, either that evening or the next day draft, review, and send through email a brief, concise, and direct thank you letter.

The thank you letter is not another interview. The thank you letter is not a tool to attach work product, more references (unless requested to do so), or anything else for that matter. What should be included is a brief introduction paragraph thanking the interviewer again for taking time to interview you for this opportunity. In a brief, concise, and direct manner restate why you believe your experience is a fit for the role as you understand it now from the interview, and communicate your level of interest in moving to the next phase of the process. Include all means of contacting you as well as best times to reach you on the phone. Advise the recipients that if that have any additional questions or information they need from you to simply call or respond to the email and you would be happy to provide the information. That is all that needs to be in a thank you letter. Again, the employer doesn't have to read, distribution, respond, or even acknowledge this communication during their recruitment process so if you go beyond this advice and start writing a novel about why you are so wonderful and why they need you it will be viewed negatively and discarded.

Many times an applicant is not provided business cards, or they only have one email address to send the thank you letter. My advice on this is to send the thank you letter to either the one contact or all contacts at the same time in one communication. If you have multiple contacts, send the email "to" all of them and address them all in the opening salutation. If you have only one contact, send the communication to the one individual, and in the salutation you still include all of the names of the people involved in the interview. Avoid at all costs sending different communications with different content to each member of the interview process without first considering the fact that they will share the emails and compare to see if there is any inconsistencies or bias taking place between the communication and interaction.

Do not wait too long to send the thank you communication. Certainly back in time when snail mail was used and the internet did not exist you could send a response a week or so later and maybe you would reconnect with the employer in due time. That is not the case today and organizations are moving at a faster pace than ever before. Same day evening, next day at the latest, but if you linger too long guess what? They will have already made a decision and if you were hoping to restate your enthusiasm and interest in the role through the thank you communication you will be too late.

CHAPTER FOURTEEN

TIPS ABOUT JOB OFFERS

When you receive the job offer, especially if it is verbal only, you will want to digest the information, review it, and take time to make the best decision for you and your family as appropriate. Do not assume all employers make their best offer to you as their first offer. At the same time, don't assume every employer makes a low offer anticipating negotiation of a higher rate or pay or salary. No two employers are exactly alike and the offer process is as much based on the person handling the offer as it is the philosophy and best practices of the company and industry.

The level and type of position you are receiving an offer for also impacts the type of negotiation power you may have and the flexibility of the employer. An entry level first job out of college will be handled on both ends of the process differently than an experienced executive or manager. What I want to instill upon you is that everything is negotiable to an extent, the end result and response to any request may be refusal or not what you want, but you may certainly ask. There are some key terms of employment you will want to discuss and satisfy your expectations including: base pay or salary, bonus eligibility, sign-on bonus, paid time off, equity, and seniority.

The base pay or salary is something you want to make sure you are comfortable with because everything else during your career with this employer will have some reference to this amount, including potentially promotions, salary increases, incentive and performance based bonuses, and even the value of earned vested paid time off. Many organizations do not have budget flexibility to increase the offered salary or match other company salary structures. That is okay, just make sure you feel fairly compensated for the work you are performing and in line with industry standards for similar experience, education, credentials, etc.

Applicants often have greater success in the private industry when asking for a sign on bonus than a higher base salary. This is because a one-time cash payout, that usually is connected to a retention payback provision, has less long term financial impact and risk to the employer than an increase in base pay. Consider the employer that pays a higher salary to each applicant who asks for it would incur increased payroll taxes, retirement plan match contributions, insurance rates could be higher for various offerings such as disability salary continuation plans, life insurance, and other benefits. Further, every raise, promotion, and other personnel activity that impacts pay will already be starting at a higher level, potentially creating internal equity challenges and fair treatment of all employees. If they provide a new employee a one-time cash payment there is minimal impact long term. That is why I suggest always taking this approach if a higher salary request is denied or does not meet your expectations.

Early on you will certainly want to make sure that you are aware of any waiting period or criteria required to be eligible for incentive or performance bonus programs. If you accept a position in August only to find out in January that you must be employed six months or more during the prior calendar year to be eligible for a bonus payment you will be very disengaged and even disgruntled if you believe you were misled.

You will want to determine how you can be granted seniority based on your experience level in the industry, and whether new or returning as an employee you want to secure an appropriate level and amount of paid time off in accordance with your total industry experience. For example, if you are leaving an employer after 12 years and earned 20 days of paid time off, you should negotiate and not settle for 10 days of paid time off with a new employer since you will almost never recover this loss in time off. Ask the new employer to grant you equivalent paid time off so you maintain your lifestyle and level of accrual. Think about it this way, they are probably hiring you because of your many years of experience. In return, you should request an appropriate amount of compensation and paid time off benefits which comes with your level of experience you have earned and they want from you. If there are any equity programs, such as stock purchase plans or stock options, be certain the information is well defined and provided to you when making your decision.

If an employer asks you to make a decision during the verbal offer discussion, advise them that you will provide a verbal acceptance only and that no relationship exists until you receive a formal written offer letter that outlines all of the conditions of employment so you can review and execute as appropriate. Most employers request verbal acceptance to then initiate the criminal background check, drug screening, motor vehicle check if appropriate, and references, seeking some commitment before proceeding. It is fine to provide that verbal acceptance, because the employer also wants protection from you being hired if any of the preceding checks result in unsatisfactory findings leading to an offer being rescinded.

Counter offers from your current employer as something to be touched upon briefly as we wrap up this book. Be cautious when playing the game of getting a new offer just to pressure your current employer into raising your compensation. Human resources professionals have been managing this game for decades and are very good at finding a way to separate you from employment once they can replace you since you have already demonstrated a desire to no longer remain with your current employer.

For example, in most organizations where employment is at-will, if you tell them you are resigning unless they pay you more money, you may get an instant raise of $10,000. Wow right? Wrong, because you will only get a month or two of the higher pay while they recruit or promote someone else into your role at the appropriate salary and you will have turned down an acceptable offer from another employer. It is easier to agree to a short term increase and find a new employee who wants to be with the employer than keep you on payroll at a higher pay, which may create inequity and pay disparity, long term. It is easier to have the work continue as is, and perform knowledge transfer activities than lose you in two weeks or less. So recognize there are strategies employers use to deal with offers, and one strategy is the counter offer. Now not all situations are as described, but it is a tool a business uses to retain a departing employee a little longer.

A new employer will not appreciate going through the process of recruiting you and making you an offer only to get involved in a salary negotiation battle due to a counter offer. In my career I always rescinded the offer and moved on to another applicant when it was determined the negotiation was less about value and equity in the role for work performed and instead a battle with their former employer. You do not want to burn bridges, and you do not want people in your industry or professional thinking you wasted their time in an effort to get a salary increase at their current employer.

With all of this said, do not hesitate to decline an offer after attempting to negotiate if you do not get what you are looking for. If you settle and you are truly not happy with the compensation and benefits package of the new company, you are already setting yourself up for a miserable existence there and will struggle to engage and feel valued.

Your job offer should include your rate of pay or salary, your Fair Labor Standards Act status of either Non-Exempt or Exempt, which signifies whether or not the position is overtime eligible. The offer should explain benefits eligibility, start date, and have attached some information on benefit programs offered and rate sheets for your review and consideration. The offer should detail what location you will work at, and what your title is with the company. There should be language about the offer being conditional upon successful completion of background check activities as noted above, and that any representation about the position, compensation, conditions of employment, or benefits made during the interview process not defined in the offer letter are not valid. Most letters will also define if the role is at-will employment. Read the offer closely and ask questions as appropriate so you are confident in what you accepting and committing to with the new employer. Happy career hunting!

CHAPTER FIFTEEN

COMMON QUESTIONS ABOUT INTERVIEWS

This final chapter is included to provide a sampling of different questions received over the years related to interviewing from applicants. These questions have been presented either during a training session, independent of training, during an interview, or just randomly over my career. While most of the answers have already been provided in this book, this is another medium to approach guidance for you, the interested reader, from a different perspective.

How do I avoid talking too much during the interview.

Focus on your preparation for the interview, listening skills, and strategy for staying aligned with the questions presented to avoid tangents. Read the body language of the interviewer and practice your responses based on interview question themes presented in this book with family and friends to improve your skills in articulating your experience and competencies.

How can I demonstrate a lack of nervousness without appearing over confident?

The employer is looking for competent responses to their inquiries, and anticipate and expect a certain level of nervousness from an applicant. Complete lack of observable nervous behavior is not an automatic indication of being over confident. Perhaps it is simply a demonstration of being prepared.

Can I ask the employer how many applicants there are?

You certainly can, however there is no real value in presenting the question or in the answer. Your performance and how well you articulate and demonstrate your skills, experience, and capabilities is not impacted by any external factor like other applicants, the number of applicants or interviews being held, and so on. You need to focus on yourself, and ensuring that you demonstrate to the employer how and why you are the best applicant for the position.

How should retirees prepare for an interview and demonstrate value to a potential employer?

The same manner in which any other applicant would present themselves based on the strategies and techniques presented in this book. There are some challenges to overcome, such as age based discrimination and a change of career in which limited prior experience is applicable. In either case the applicant should apply the teaching of this book and focus their responses on demonstrating their qualifications against the minimum requirements of the position. Similarly, retirees should not expect to be hired just because of the cumulative "work" experience they have. Like any other applicant, they must demonstrate the ability to perform the essential functions of the role. Some employers may emphasize the physical demands of the position, so retirees should pay close attention to any information they can obtain regarding the actual physical requirements and be sure they meet the requirements before applying.

How do you present skills you haven't used in a recent job?

As discussed in this book, when reviewing the job posting and examining the required qualifications for the position, you must identify for yourself what tasks you have direct experience in performing and what tasks you have transferrable skills to learn and master. By examining the latter you will use the interview planning and preparation time to make notes of how you performed similar tasks in other roles so you can build your responses with factual honest information regarding what your competence and capabilities are related to those essential functions that you have no direct prior experience performing. It will be up to the employer to determine from how well you articulate the correlation if the experience is actually transferrable and applicable to the position for which you applied. Also, keep in mind that the employer should have reviewed your resume, and considering this fact they still decided to interview you. If you haven't performed a task in many years and your resume or application demonstrated that fact, then they already are aware of the gap in time since you have done that type of work and will probably ask questions relevant to how you would refresh your ability to perform similar tasks now.

Thank you for taking time to read this book. I trust there was adequate information applicable to your goals and objectives as an applicant now or in the future to gain value from the content. These have been practical strategies, techniques, and perspectives that if executed and implemented will result in a more comprehensive and successful interview process and experience for you. I wish you tremendous success in reaching all of your career aspirations.

SymbianceHR, LLC

SymbianceHR delivers over twenty years of human capital management expertise in private and public.

We align our strategic human capital management, business experience, and alliance partners with your organizational needs to deliver customized solutions and services to achieve established business goals.

When you engage our services you don't have to look any further for human capital management services from anywhere else. From the first hire until the last separation SymbianceHR is your consultant and advisor able to provide directly or through our strategic partners all of the services and solutions you need or want. Our approach and process saves you time, money, and achieves compliance for your business.

Visit our website at http:///www.symbiancehr.net to download bonus materials. The bonus material is a reference guide based on the strategies, tips, and techniques presented in this book.

ABOUT THE AUTHOR

Warren S. Cook is a human capital strategic management consultant with over twenty years of experience across various industries in both private and public sectors.

He is the Director of Consulting Services and Managing Member of SymbianceHR, LLC based out of Wilmington, DE where he provides human capital consulting to small and mid-sized companies to help them achieve business success. Warren resides in Chesapeake City, Maryland with his wife Jennifer and children.

When not consulting or writing, Warren and Jennifer enjoy traveling around the United States, gardening, swimming, biking, and spending quality time with the family.